CONTENTS

PREFACE 3
1. INTRODUCTION 4
2. WHY DO I WRITE ABOUT THE 737 MAX? 6
3. AIRCRAFT STALL 8
   QUESTION: What is aircraft stall? 8
   QUESTION: Why is aircraft stall SO important to the 737 MAX? 8
   QUESTION: How can a pilot detect aircraft stall? 9
4. LION AIR JT610 – CRASH 14
5. LION AIR JT610 – RECENT HISTORY 21
6. AOA DISAGREE & RUNAWAY TRIM 24
   QUESTION: Why did Lion Air replace the original AOA sensor? 28
   QUESTION: Why change the TRIM switch function? 30
   QUESTION: What is important about these two TRIM switches? ... 30
7. ETHIOPIAN AIR FLIGHT ET302 33
   QUESTION: Did both flight crews do everything right? 41
8. WHY MCAS? 44
   QUESTION: What are the physical essentials of MCAS software? ... 45
   QUESTION: Why did they need to modify a 737, and not start on a new design? 50
9. WHAT DOES MCAS ACTUALLY DO? 55
   QUESTION: Why didn't Boeing have MCAS work on a gradual sliding scale? 56
10. MCAS SOFTWARE – FLIGHT CRITICAL 66
    QUESTION: How many 737 MAX flight hours were logged before the first crash (JT610)? 69
    QUESTION: Should MCAS software be classified as Catastrophic? ... 69
11. HOW FLIGHT CONTROLS WORK 74
12. WHAT IS LONGITUDINAL INSTABILITY? 81
    QUESTION: Why did Boeing allow this 4th generation 737 MAX airplane to have unsteady Pitch? 82
13. REDESIGN OF 737 INTO 737 MAX 8 83

14. **FULL FLIGHT SIMULATOR TRAINING SHOULD BE REQUIRED** 92

    QUESTION: Does the 737 NG flight simulator display the "AOA Disagree" warning? 93

    QUESTION: Can pilots tell if their airplane is going into a stall without AOA sensors? 95

15. **Federal aviation administration** 99

    BRIEF HISTORY 99

    ODA's 100

    BOEING OVERSIGHT 103

    F.A.A. MANAGEMENT – APPROVING DOCUMENTATION 104

    F.A.A. MANAGEMENT – INACTION 106

    F.A.A. MANAGEMENT BAD DECISONS 107

    SLEEPING WITH BOEING? 110

    QUESTION: If Boeing has only 950 AR inspectors, why would the F.A.A. need 10,000 more manufacturing ASI's? 113

16. **MCAS - FLAWS** 115

17. **BOEING's PRELIMINARY FIX** 118

    QUESTION: How important is a Runaway Trim procedure? 120

18. **A REAL FIX** 126

    More than a Single Point of Failure 126

    Redundancy 129

    Full Motion Flight Simulator Training 130

    Investigate MCAS software Development 131

    Sliding Scale 133

    Other Ideas to Make the 737 MAX Safe 134

    Lottery 135

19. **WHAT DID BOEING KNOW AND WHEN did they know?** 136

20. **MEETINGS / INVESTIGATIONS** 142

    QUESTION: Why didn't Boeing change the MCAS software, after finding it had an error, for the newly manufactured 737 MAX airplanes? 142

21.	**ODDS & ENDS**..151	
22.	**CONCLUSIONS**..158	
	Criminals 158	
	Poor Design and Implementation 159	
	MCAS Disabled or Fails..161	
	Problems to Correct with the F.A.A. 162	
	Other Obvious Matters 163	
	QUESTION: Is Boeing too big to fail?...163	
	Lawsuits...163	
23.	**GLOSSARY** 167	

Copyright © 2019 by Dennis J. Coughlin.
First published in 2019.

PREFACE

Boeing's design of the 737 Max has a problem, it cannot fly without the Maneuvering Characteristics Augmentation System (MCAS) software; it cannot be disabled, because then the aircraft becomes unairworthy.

The jet engines had to be placed differently on the 737 MAX because they could not be fitted under the wings as was done on the original 737. New CFM LEAP 1B jet engines needed to be mounted higher and farther forward to achieve needed ground clearance. Doing so shifted the center of gravity nearer to the center of lift, creating a new aircraft design that is longitudinally unstable (it tends to force the nose up in flight).

Boeing engineers created MCAS software to avoid nose up conditions, by using an automated Pitch Trim system to counteract longitudinal instability.

To fully automate MCAS: Boeing engineers removed all Pitch Trim pilot safeguards; then after flight testing, in MCAS software, they changed the limits without notifying the F.A.A.; and Boeing wrongly classified MCAS software from their own "internal" System Safety Analysis, as only "hazardous" not "catastrophic". It caused two plane crashes; all 346 lives were lost, definitely a "catastrophic" system needing redundancy.

I want to thank Dominic Gates of the Seattle Times, his articles inspired me to research this topic and write a book on the 737 MAX airplanes.

1. INTRODUCTION

Any person reading this should know something about my background. My work in aviation spans 42 years.

Let me start all the way back in 1977, when I first started in avionics (electronics in aviation) in the U.S. Air Force Reserve (activated for 1.5 years 1980 – 1981). Although I have dabbled in other electronic fields of endeavor when I was a reservist, when hired into civil service back in 1981, I began my full-time avionics life.

When I retired from civil service, I was a GS-856-13 (Avionics Technician, GS-13). To anyone outside the government, those letters and numbers are meaningless, so let me put that in perspective. A lawyer who had passed the bar exam and argued cases in a courtroom, or a journeyman engineer with a bachelor's degree and experience, would be hired into the government at the GS-13 grade level. Put a different way, a mission specialist on a spacecraft funded by NASA is normally a GS-14 grade level, and they will have at least one PhD, plus experience in their field of study.

A full resume of mine describing everything I've done in the aviation world would take multiple pages. Suffice it to say, I've done just about every job that an Avionics Technician can do. In my 42 years, I've seen everything from experimental aircraft to the wide-body Boeing 747, and almost everything in-between. I've done bench repair work, flight line maintenance and debriefing of pilots. I've been an instructor, field engineer, inspector, programmer, and aircraft I.T. server technician. I've scheduled inspections, performed calibrations, worked with test equipment, automatic test equipment (ATE), aircraft ground equipment (AGE), worked in a battery shop, worked with simulators, and assisted A&P's on mechanical / engines / fuel / air conditioning / sheet metal /etc.

Anyone who reads this book can skip to whatever chapter interests them, if they only need knowledge on a specific subject. I wrote the book so a reader wanting to jump to any chapter can do it, but in so doing I have had to repeat some basic facts so jumping around in my book is possible. However, many chapters have additional topics that I use to help flow from one chapter to the next, so it's an easy read.

When I was an Avionics Instructor at the FAA Academy in Oklahoma City, I taught a class of Airworthiness Safety Inspectors on the concept of windshear, not knowing that one of my students had lost a daughter in the airplane crash I was describing. It was a humbling moment, as he had more information than I had…So, I try and do as much exhaustive research BEFORE writing a final work.

In aviation plenty of terms and acronyms are used; at the end of my book are pages devoted to explaining those I use.

Please consider this as only Volume I. Once the full story unravels, I will release a new book, Volume II, on what will be revealed from all of the various investigations into Boeing, and their deadly product, the 737 MAX. Not an exaggeration, 346 people died due to Boeing's aircraft design.

2. WHY DO I WRITE ABOUT THE 737 MAX?

There have been 2 horrific crashes of commercial airliners (Boeing 737 MAX 8) causing 346 people to die, each death can be blamed on the Maneuvering Characteristics Augmentation System (MCAS) software; it was NOT pilot error that ended so many lives.

Both aircraft were doomed by design. Failures by Boeing employees and Collins Aerospace contributed to the loss of individual lives and the devastation wrought on their families, across multiple continents. The Federal Aviation Administration (F.A.A.) managers did their best to ensure an unsafe aircraft was certified for carrying passengers, while also insisting pilots did not need to know about MCAS. Managers from Boeing and those at the F.A.A. need to be individually prosecuted for negligent homicide, they all had different roles to play and were significant contributors to both crashes.

After researching each crash and how Boeing created MCAS software, and its authorization by the F.A.A., it is my opinion that criminal negligence can be proved beyond a reasonable doubt, from the facts about the design and certification of the Boeing 737 MAX aircraft.

Never in the history of man has anything even approached the level of callousness and greed shown by management to mass produce a deadly product, on purpose, other than Zyklon B.

I have an urgency to make the public aware of the problems about the 737 MAX. If Boeing is as successful selling that series of aircraft as it has plans to do, it could account for up to 8,000 flights a day in the U.S., before it ceases production. That's 3 million flights each year just in the U.S., so a once in a million chance will occur – 3 times a year! And, the U.S. market is forecast to account for just 25% of the world-wide 737 MAX sales.

In a related note, AirSafe.com reports that a fatal crash, among all 737's being flown today, have a rate of 0.23 per million flights.[1] To unpack that statement, if there are 4 million flights of current 737 airplanes world-wide, then one of them will result in fatalities every year.

When the entire world is factored in, there is only 1 fatal aircraft crash for every 3 million flights[2] for all types of commercial aircraft flown. Add 75% of the 737 MAX fleet will be flown by foreign carriers, and the odds of another 737 MAX crash are a certainty, unless it is fixed properly, with redundancy – two functioning and active MCAS per plane (not just using two AOA sensors feeding a single MCAS system).

To sum it up, I wrote this book for anyone who flies in a commercial airplane, or has a loved one who does; to equip them with knowledge when choosing an airplane to ride in.

Some readers will already know a few facts on each crash, but I will go into detail after a few brief explanations. Official, final documentation, on both crash investigations are months, if not years away. (This book was completed in August 2019.)

---

[1] Washington Post, " 'Safety was just a given': Inside Boeing's boardroom amid the 737 MAX crisis ", Douglas MacMillan, 5/5/2019
Quartz, "Boeing's cold-blooded risk calculation may tarnish trust in 'self-driving' cars for years, Michael J. Cohen, 4/10/2019

3. AIRCRAFT STALL

QUESTION: WHAT IS AIRCRAFT STALL?

Simply put, civilian commercial airplanes use engines to produce thrust, making the aircraft move forward. As the forward movement increases, wind above the wings creates a vacuum (66%), and wind below the wings creates pressure (33%). Once the total lift exceeds the weight of the aircraft, it achieves flight. Pressure underneath the wings helps achieve flight, but it works against the aircraft in a stall.

Stall occurs when the trailing edge of the wings no longer have enough smooth air flowing over them. When the speed and pitch angle of the aircraft combine to disrupt the airflow over the trailing edge of the wing, it does not have enough lift to overcome its weight, and gravity makes it return to Earth – quickly. In the case of the 737 MAX 8, it typically weighs 180,000 lbs. on take-off. Falling tail first back to Earth because of a stall, well, it needs to be avoided.

Considering the size, shape and weight of the 737 MAX, a stall in-flight would be catastrophic.

Every airplane can stall, at any speed, if it exceeds the critical Angle of Attack (which is the point of maximum lift). It all depends on Center of Gravity, winds aloft, outside air temperature, altitude, and changes in engine thrust.

QUESTION: WHY IS AIRCRAFT STALL SO IMPORTANT TO THE 737 MAX?

MCAS is software in the Flight Control Computer (FCC), it adjusts the pitch of the aircraft automatically, so the 737 MAX never stalls in flight. One primary input to MCAS software is the Angle of Attack sensor. (*Electrically, signals from the AOA sensor feed the Air Data*

Computer / Air Data Inertial Reference Unit, and it then sends a digital word for AOA data to the FCC.)

Not to gloss over all of the other functions the FCC's perform, because they control most movable surfaces on the 737 MAX exterior. Boeing used to believe in redundancy for safety, before focusing lately on profits. Back in 2003 when the basic principles of the FCC were conceived by Boeing, each 737 needed two of them.[3] On top of even that, inside it are 2 different CPU's, one from Intel, the other from AMD.

There is no MCAS Circuit Breaker to pull to disable the system, it is integral to the FCC.

Looking at the glass cockpit, pilots can see the pitch of the aircraft on their attitude displays, as well as the airspeed and altitude. However, that is meaningless when it comes to figuring out when stall is going to occur.

Boeing designed the 737 MAX to be longitudinally unstable; doing so increases the fuel efficiency. But that also has the effect to pitch the nose up occasionally.

MCAS software was originally invented to take control of the pitch axis of the aircraft, and override pilot commands, to keep the 737 MAX from stalling.

QUESTION: HOW CAN A PILOT DETECT AIRCRAFT STALL?

All previous 737 aircraft had some type of AOA dial gage indicators displayed in the cockpit, linked to external AOA sensors. Some manager at Boeing decided to sell these indicators for $80,000 on each aircraft, as part of an "Error Notification Kit" to the glass cockpit, another revenue generator for Boeing. Better customers such as

---

[3] Satcom guru (website), "Stabilizer Trim", Peter Lemme, 11/12/2018

Southwest were offered this same option at $50,000[4] (probably the cost of adding AOA Indicator without amber AOA disagree light.)

It's hard to understand the logic behind this action, not displaying the AOA Indicators. Pilots have but one way to determine if the aircraft they are flying is *approaching* a stall condition, by looking at the AOA gages. (If you don't believe me, ask a pilot to calculate stall – give them a 737 MAX 8 aircraft: total weight, CG, speed, altitude, and pitch angle – see if they can answer when the aircraft would exceed stall? Don't give them vertical winds aloft, if they answer, they are lying.)

Some pilots remark that they can "feel" when an aircraft is stalling (not *approaching* a stall). Any pilot that has an IFR rating knows they cannot rely on their feelings but must rely on their aircraft instruments.

An example of a pilot who relied on his feelings is John F. Kennedy Jr., he ignored his instruments when all of the landmarks he was using became obscured by hazy conditions. The weather conditions were poor, but an experienced pilot could file a VFR flight plan. On July 16, 1999, he crashed his Piper Saratoga airplane into the sea, his wife and her sister died along with him. NTSB attributed the crash to Spatial Distortion,[5] a condition where a pilot loses situation awareness; he/she cannot determine their position, location, or the MOTION of the aircraft.

A pilot is never to trust his/her feelings as a precise motion-detecting-system when steering an airplane; that is why most commercial airplanes have an AOA Indicator. (Truly fly-by-wire airplanes don't need an AOA Indicator because the flight computer calculates stall for them.)

Boeing took and made stall prevention autonomous, taking stall prevention out of the pilot's hands, made the AOA Indicators a pricey

---

[4] Wall Street Journal, "Between Two Deadly Crashes, Boeing Moved Haltingly to Make 737 MAX Fixes", Andy Pasztor, Andrew Tangel and Alison Sider, 4/1/2019
[5] NTSB Final Report, NYC99MA178, 7/6/2000

option. Only 20% of their customers paid to have these indicators displayed in their cockpits.[6]

On a related note, Boeing made it a standard requirement on all 737 MAX airplanes with MCAS software, that an **AOA DISAGREE** warning be displayed in the glass cockpit whenever the AOA sensors disagreed by 10° for ten seconds.

However, the people at Collins Aerospace writing the software code for MCAS tied that AOA warning to the pricey option of displaying the AOA Indicators. So, 80% of Boeing 737 MAX customers did not have that required warning, including Lion Air and Ethiopian Air.

In my research I've been able to easily find 80 instances where AOA sensor failures/problems in the past decade or so happened on commercial airplanes. Bird strikes, lightning, and a whole host of other things can damage the AOA sensors. One database that keeps track of bird strikes on aircraft noted there have been 1,172 instances, with 122 affecting the AOA sensors since 1990.[7] Not having the budget that CNN has, they found in the F.A.A.'s Service Difficulty Reporting database 216 instances where the AOA sensor had problems on commercial aircraft in the past decade or so.[8]

An AOA sensor failure on the Cirrus SF50 Vision Jet had grounded the whole fleet.[9] The F.A.A. issued an emergency Airworthiness Directive, AD 2019-08-05 because there were 3 incidents (no crashes)

---

[6] New York Times, Boeing Believed a 737 Max Warning Light Was Standard. It Wasn't", David Gelles and Natalie Kitroeff, 5/5/2019

[7] New York Times, "Boeing Built Deadly Assumptions Into 737 MAX, Blind to a Late Design Change", Jack Nicas, Natalie Kitroeff, David Gelles, and James Glanz, 6/1/2019

[8] CNN, "Boeing relied on single sensor for 737 Max that had been flagged 216 times to FAA", Curt Devine and Drew Griffin, 4/30/2019

[9] Aviation Today, "FAA Grounds Cirrus Vision Jets After Angle of Attack Incidents", Woodrow Bellamy III, 4/29/2019

of where the set screw on its internal mechanism was not tightened down at the factory.

   Currently, there is no other way for a pilot to know if they are approaching a stall condition, without the AOA Indicators. Vertical winds aloft can vary when any aircraft is approaching a stall condition. There is no other way to detect an impending stall, without an external AOA sensor today. Commercial airplanes fly in the Jet Stream that is constantly changing.

   My former supervisor was flying in a small jet aircraft with dual engines, as they took off in 90° heat, the aircraft hit a goose on take-off. More specifically, the bird was ingested by one engine causing it to flame out. Very few small corporate aircraft can continue to climb if one engine "flames out" during take-off, but this was supposed to one of those powerful aircraft; total weight of the aircraft in high heat and low pressure atmospheric conditions caused it to land sooner than the flight crew ever anticipated.

   He told me he could feel himself sinking, definitely true, as the airplane did land on a golf course that was just beyond the end of the runway. He had no ESP ability to predetermine a stall condition, but he definitely knew **when** it did happen.

   One funny story I do remember of that accident was how he opened the emergency exit door of that corporate jet after landing on the 16th fairway, and then he flung it farther than any high schooler could throw a shotput, over 50 feet. His fear must have poured all his available adrenaline into his heart at once, to chuck a 20 lbs. exit door that distance (there were no fatalities).

   Pilots have always been the primary failsafe whenever an aircraft goes into stall. Stated another way, stall prevention is a pilot function. Those two statements have been true for every Boeing aircraft ever built before the 737 MAX. None of those previously built aircraft were prone to a stall. Boeing removed all STAB TRIM safeguards, took the prevention of a stall out of the pilot's hands, and made it automatic – without telling the pilots, on a plane designed to become unstable at high speeds.

No commercial airplanes used to haul passengers is prone to stall, all other manufactured airplanes are stable.

Whether you're a lighter than air pilot (hot air balloons or blimps), private pilot, or professional pilot, you all know about winds aloft. Up drafts and down drafts near mountains, turbulence, storms, or changes in the jet stream; all of them will cause changes in the wind speed and direction.[10] Everyday winds aloft will be different even if a pilot flies the same route over and over, every day. And changes will occur at different altitudes too, even on the same spot on Earth. How the outside air that is sweeping across the wings (and nacelles in the 737 MAX) will change where the critical angle of attack is on the 737 MAX.

---

[10] National Geographic, "What is turbulence – and how can you calm down about it", Michelle Z. Donahue

4. LION AIR JT610 – CRASH

Lion Air Flight JT610 crashed on October 29, 2018, killing all 181 passengers and 8 crew members. Instead of landing at Pangkal Pinang, Indonesia, it crashed into the Java Sea.

The aircraft that crashed was a Boeing 737 Max 8, originally delivered to Lion Air in August 2018 and had approximately 900 hours of flight time on the airframe when it went down. Its Captain was a 31-year-old veteran with 5,000 hours of flight time in a 737; his First Officer was also experienced, he was 41 years old, and had 4,000 hours flight time on the 737 as well.

The Republic of Indonesia refers to this flight as LNI610 in their Preliminary Report on the accident (that was the airplane's call sign when talking to ATC).

Lift-off occurred on October 29, 2018, at 6:20 AM local time (23:20.40 UTC), from Soekarno-Hatta International Airport, 32 feet above sea level; that airport services Jakarta and the surrounding area. Time elapsed from when JT610 took off until it crashed was 11 minutes and 22 seconds.

Horizontal stabilizer Pitch Trim was set at 6.5 units, by the pilots before the take-off roll.

PIC refers to Pilot in Command, and SIC stands for Second in Command. (Captain = PIC, First Officer = SIC.) **AND** stands for Automatic Nose Down command from software inside the FCC.

	Lion Air Flight JT610 Timeline
23:20:36	• Captain's Stick Shaker activates (constant vibration and noise above 85 dB)
23:20:40	• Weight on Wheels switch indicates JT610 leaving the runway • JT610 climbed at a rate of 1,500 ft/min • **MASTER CAUTION** illuminates (possibly because of AOA sensors disagreeing)
23:22:05	• ATC tracks altitude of JT610, it's at 2,150 ft.
23:22:31	• MCAS activates for 10 seconds, AND (Automatic Nose Down) command • JT610 loses 2.5 units of trim (pilots fight to keep trim at 4 units) • JT610 altitude is approximately 2,300 ft.
23:22:46	• Pilot pushes **MASTER CAUTION** indicator/switch, no longer illuminated
23:22:49	• Stick Shaker quits vibration and noise
23:22:55	• MCAS starts to activate a second time, another *AND* command
23:22:56	• SIC contacts ATC and asks for airspeed check (322 knots)
23:22:59	• Pilot sets flaps to 5° • MCAS is stopped by flaps extending • JT610 altitude has dropped approximately 700 ft (altitude is 1,600 ft.) • JT610 airspeed is 300 knots
23:23:04	• Stick Shaker starts again and is active for the rest of the flight
23:23:16	• Five short *AND* commands for next few seconds (Speed Trim system?)
23:24:50	• Pilots retard engine throttles • JT610 reaches 5,300 ft., and it gains and loses altitude in a rollercoaster motion as pilots battle MCAS for control, until the end of the Flight

23:25:18	<ul><li>Flaps fully retracted</li><li>JT610 altitude is 5,200 ft.</li><li>JT610 airspeed is 250 knots</li></ul>
23:25:39	<ul><li>MCAS is activated, and continues *AND* commands (25 times) until end of flight, pilots try and counter with Pitch Trim thumb switches multiple times</li></ul>
23:29:28	<ul><li>**MASTER CAUTION** illuminates for 5 seconds before a pilot pushes on it and turns it off</li></ul>
23:31:05	<ul><li>Pilots lose tug-o-war with MCAS</li></ul>
23:31:09	<ul><li>PIC contacts ATC and says he is unable to determine airspeed</li></ul>
23:31:58	<ul><li>JT610 impacts with Java Sea</li></ul>

A few seconds prior to lift-off happening, the flight crew was already in trouble, the Captain's Stick Shaker went off and started flooding the cockpit with noise before the Weight-on-Wheels switch had shown gears-up. (Having already exceeding V1 speed, JT610 was committed to flight.) Although both Stick Shakers are also tied to their individual AOA sensors, they are completely independent from MCAS.

Because of how the AOA sensor affects both altitude and airspeed readings, the Captain's altimeter showed it was quite higher than the First Officers'. ATC was contacted about 45 seconds after being airborne, and the First Officer asks them for an altitude check, they were only at 900 ft.

Both **MASTER CAUTION** switches illuminated while the flaps were being retracted, and it took almost one minute for one of the pilots to press it to extinguish that light. (I don't know what triggered this indicator/switch to illuminate.) **MASTER CAUTION** illuminated again at the end of the flight; about the time they went pitch down/nose down for the fifth time.

Flight JT610 still maintained a steady rate of climb. Airspeed was approximately 225 knots whereas the altitude was close to 1,800 ft. (above ground level), before MCAS took control.

The initial command from MCAS was 10 seconds long, and it decreased the Pitch Trim by about 2.5 units, forcing the horizontal stabilizer to be close to 4 units.

MCAS would command Pitch Trim down (automatic nose down = *AND*) of the horizontal stabilizer, afterwards the pilots would counter MCAS by using the Pitch Trim thumb switches on top of the yoke in the cockpit, to command Pitch Trim up (automatic nose up = *ANU*).

Both the pilots and MCAS made +20 pitch commands, yet, that does not tell the whole story. Every time the pilots would use the Pitch Trim thumb switches on the yoke, it reset MCAS, allowing it to command another 2.5° *AND* command, instead of MCAS follow-up commands being only 0.5°.

Pilot action cut out MCAS quite a few times, because the thumb switches forcing *ANU*, would stop the horizontal stabilizer from taking commands from MCAS, but, had the unintended consequence of resetting MCAS.

Probably the most troubling aspect of this tug-o-war with a "ghost" – was the pilots did not know they needed to push on the yoke thumb switches longer, commanding *ANU*, for the same duration MCAS had given an *AND* command. So, the aircraft gained airspeed, even after the pilot retarded the throttles because the aircraft kept pointing down so much, over and over, as pilots fought to go nose up repeatedly.

As the pilots fought for vertical control, they began a tug-o-war with MCAS, causing the aircraft to start to porpoise (altitude fluctuated up and down). Fighting between MCAS and the pilots took the rest of the flight.

It is very evident the Captain was trying everything he knew to avoid a crash, he even tried extending the flaps to see if that helped, if the crude FDR graph in the Indonesian Aircraft Investigation Preliminary Report is accurate. Doing so stopped MCAS from exercising commands while the flaps were extended to 5°.

Because the Captain had to page through a paper manual on NON-NORMAL CHECHLISTS to see if any applied, it took time he did not have. (Putting down the flaps at high speed is not recommended, but the Captain was trying to fight to save the airplane.)

One minute before the crash the Captain called ATC to get an airspeed check, because of the disparity in airspeed readings between him and the First Officer's airspeed indications, caused by the Captain's AOA sensor being 20° off. When he radioed ATC, he gave the wrong call sign (LNI650 instead of LNI610), an evident factor that the flight crew was under extreme stress. ATC radioed back that "LNI610" was proceeding at 322 knots IAS.

One forgotten fact, every time the 737 MAX 8 pitched down in altitude, the pilots would be looking at the ground (or the Java Sea) if they looked through the cockpit windshield. Besides adding to the stress level in the cockpit of what they saw, the passengers would feel this pitching up and down like a bad rollercoaster ride. Passengers must have experienced terrifying thoughts that something was wrong, not knowing exactly what was making their flight erratic, unable to help, realizing that they were in danger.

Any passenger who has flown before probably experienced turbulence, but never that close to the ground, immediately after take-off. Not only were the pilot's hand-flying the 737 MAX 8, but besides that rocky turbulence, add to it the ups and downs of a rollercoaster.

What the pilots could not recognize was what they were fighting. MCAS was unknown to them. It was as if they were fighting a ghost making these pitch down commands.

Don't forget those were humans on board Flight JT610, people with future hopes and dreams, just wanting to get from point "A" to point "B". If you focus only on facts and numbers, you lose the most important aspect of this tragedy, 189 humans beings lost their lives at the same time.

**A tragedy like this should never happen again!
(but it did)**

Pilots in the U.S. have done a tremendous disservice to the courageous flight crew of Lion Air JT610, disparaging them because they did not keep the airplane to a slower airspeed. Did it cross these pilot's minds that this flight crew was fighting MCAS software that gave multiple pitch down signals? Slowing the aircraft down would result in a further pitch down of the aircraft that was just above ground level.

Finally, the laws of physics did kick in, where the wind forces at high speed forced the elevators into a neutral position (elevator blowback), even though both pilots were pulling back on the yokes as hard as they could, in the end it had no effect. Once that happened, elevator blowback, for the next minute MCAS kept giving pitch down commands the pilots couldn't counter because their yoke controls failed.

When the aircraft crashed into the Java Sea, 11 minutes, 22 seconds after take-off, it was exceeding 450 knots; there were no survivors.

This was the first, but not last crash, of the 737 MAX 8, occurring within 18 months of its initial delivery to the airlines.

Even though a rescue diver lost his life while working the JT610 crash site in the Java Sea, his death is not counted in the number of deaths attributed to the airplane crash.[11]

---

[11] Reuters, "Senior Indonesian rescue diver dies in jet crash search", Tabita Diela and Agustinus Beo Da Costa, 11/3/18

5. LION AIR JT610 – RECENT HISTORY

On October 27, 2018, the Captain's AOA sensor was replaced after Lion Air flight JT775. It flew three more short flights that day. One flight was without incident, two more had AOA problems (flight JT776 – bad AOA, flight JT 2748 – no AOA problems, flight JT 2749 – bad AOA). Then on October 28, 2018, one day before the crash, that same aircraft flew some more short hops (flight JT 828 – no AOA problems, flight JT 829 – no AOA problems, flight JT043 – bad AOA).

This proves that MCAS seems to randomly pick which AOA sensor will be used before each flight. Another technical issue must also be highlighted, when the controls of the aircraft were transferred to the First Officer, MCAS software kept relying on the Captain's AOA sensor, even after switching.

Of course, MCAS really does not switch which AOA sensor to use. In the 737 NG each time the aircraft is powered-up, it would choose a different FCC to use; that is the case in the 737 MAX, that MCAS does not randomly select the AOA sensor to use, but when applying power to the 737 MAX it varies which FCC is to be primary / active.

The left AOA sensor is wired into FCC #1 system, and the right AOA sensor is wired into the FCC #2 system.

It leads to the conclusion that pilots were not writing down discrepancies observed in flight into the aircraft logbook, so maintenance could correctly diagnose the malfunction.

Pilots tend to want to fly and log flight hours, and management needs the aircraft to meet its flying schedule, so the airline makes money. It's in everyone's best interest to keep hauling passengers.

"Pocket write-ups" are the term used by flight crews to take care of defects occurring in flight. A pilot will write down on paper the malfunctions observed and then puts the paper in his/her pocket. When this technique functions without human error, the pilot gives this piece of paper to the next crew to fly the airplane. At the end of the day, all "pocket write-ups" are supposed to be put down on the aircraft logbook for maintenance to address before the next scheduled flight the following day.

Management has implemented a Minimum Equipment List, and a Deferral List, to encourage pilots to write-up all discrepancies when they occur. But, when the obvious solution to the malfunction grounds the plane from flying, then a "pocket write-up" is normally used by pilots, if they determine the defect is not safety critical to them.

On a side note, I taught F.A.A. Airworthiness Safety Inspectors (ASI's) who would sit in the cockpit jump seat and monitor the flight crews in action, called an "En Route" inspection. My instructions to them was to look for any equipment malfunctions and see if one of the pilots wrote the discrepancy down in the aircraft logbook. It was my job to try and get all of the ASI's in the U.S. to follow the same procedures when they performed an "En Route" inspections.

My initial theory, having the experience I do, is that the replaced Captain's AOA sensor was bad on Lion Air flight JT610. It was an overhauled part, the repairs done in a shop located in Miramar, Florida.

AOA sensors, like the one on the Boeing 737 MAX, normally use a "synchro transmitter" (or a potentiometer in smaller aircraft) as their internal mechanism. Located inside the case of most commercial airplanes AOA sensors is the synchro transmitter, it is very possible the mechanism was 20° off, pitch up, before it was installed. A technician is supposed to tighten down the internal mechanism, and it's entirely likely this was not done sufficiently. Either it was set inaccurately, or not tightened down all the way and moved a little bit during shipment.

Digital AOA sensors still have an internal mechanism that changes physical movement into a digital signal, all done internally. Normally the moving internal mechanism is a potentiometer, and it is part of a circuit that then translates that physical movement into digital words.

6. AOA DISAGREE & RUNAWAY TRIM

Two days before the crash, on October 27, 2018, one of the two Angle of Attack (AOA) sensors were replaced (Captain's side) after Lion Air flight JT775. But I do not believe the AOA sensor was tested in accordance to Boeing Aircraft Maintenance Manual (AMM) for the 737 MAX, Chapter 34-21-05-801.[12] According to that chapter the AOA sensor is moved physically on the exterior of the aircraft with a test jig to monitor its angle, and then checked against its cockpit information displayed. In the past I have done this inspection/test of the AOA sensor on the Boeing 737. If a single Avionics Technician (sometimes called an engineer in foreign cultures) performs this task, it is time consuming.

In the Boeing 737 MAX 8, without a glass cockpit display of the AOA gage (which Lion Air did not have) it becomes a difficult task. The "engineer" must navigate through a complex maze of instructions on the MFD (Multi-Function Display) in the cockpit to get the exact AOA sensor reading and compare it to what he set the external AOA sensor to.

Why do I believe the AOA sensor was not tested after replacement? On the flight before the crash, JT043, the FDR (Flight Data Recorder) showed that the AOA sensor replaced had a 20° error, almost identical to the recorded error on flight JT610.

An **AOA DISAGREE** warning was supposed to be standard with MCAS software. It was theoretically going to show up on the Electronic Instrument Flight System (EFIS), called the glass cockpit, whenever the two AOA sensors disagreed by 10° for 10 seconds.

---

[12] Satcom Guru (website), "Taking the Next Steps while Awaiting on the Preliminary Report from ET302", Peter Lemme, 3/24/2019

People get confused when talking about the AOA warnings, because there are two of them in the 737 MAX. One is triggered when a disparity of 5.5° between both AOA sensors, and an amber stand-alone light is illuminated in the cockpit. This is a non-essential safety option, costing up to an additional $30,000[13] as it is independent from MCAS.

The other one that engineers at Boeing noticed missing was the AOA DISAGREE warning (before September of 2017),[14] after delivery of the first few 737 MAX airplanes in the summer of 2017. The cost of correcting this software defect would delay deliveries and cost significant money to fix those already delivered. Boeing managers handpicked an internal committee[15] to give the answer they wanted to hear; i.e., no fix was needed. In this first committee's Problem Report, Boeing engineers considered this to only be "advisory" in nature, so there was no need to inform the F.A.A.[16] (After the crash of JT610, Boeing did give to the F.A.A. this Problem Report.) Cockpits have a color code to them, red means WARNING, yellow means ▓▓▓▓▓▓▓, green means NORMAL, and blue means ADVISORY, non-essential to flight; however, the AOA DISAGREE is in yellow, not blue.

Even more damning is after Boeing knew about the software problem in 2017, their plan to update MCAS with a software fix was scheduled to occur with the launch of the new 737 MAX 10, in 2020.[17]

If Lion Air had this standard warning in their 737 MAX aircraft, then pilots would have seen it on 3 previous flights, and maintenance would have fixed it. Logically, that means if the AOA DISAGREE

---

[13] VOX, "Boeing's effort to get the 737 Max approved to fly again, explained", Matthew Yglesias, 5/5/2019

[14] Reuters, "Boeing did not disclose 737 MAX alert issue to FAA for 13 months", Tracy Rucinski and David Shepardson, 5/5/2019

[15] The Washington Post, "Boeing waited until after Indonesian plane crash to inform FAA of 737 safety review", Aaron Greg, 5/5/2019

[16] Washington Post, "FAA chief pilot says pilot decisions contributed to Boeing 737 Max crashes", Micheal Laris, Lori Aratani and Ashley Halsey III, 5/15/2019

[17] Reuters, "Boeing delayed fix of defective 737 MAX warning light for three years: U.S. lawmakers", Eric M. Johnson, 6/7/2019

standard warning was displayed, Lion Air flight JT610 would not have crashed.

Having been an Avionics Technician, I also know of another thing the AOA DISAGREE should have done if the software was written correctly. There are two types of very prominent indicator lights at the very top of the Instrument panel in the cockpit, MASTER CAUTION and MASTER WARNING, one pair for the Captain, another pair for the First Officer.

> *(Older 737's have this pair, however it is my understanding the 737 MAX might not have the MASTER WARNING indicator switches. Instead it is replaced by another red switch/indicator)*

Any one of these safety annunciators will trigger the Master Caution/Warning system. Caution indicators are yellow in color, signifying a condition where there is a problem that needs to be addressed by one of the pilots very soon. Any caution light will trigger the MASTER CAUTION indicator/switches (one on the Captain's side, the other on the First Officer's side). This annunciator can only be reset if either pilot pushes the MASTER CAUTION indicator switches.

Warning indicators are red, when illuminated they specify a failure condition and require immediate attention from the pilot in command. A warning light will trigger the indicator/switches (one on Captains side, the other on the First Officers side). This annunciator can only be reset if either pilot pushes the MASTER WARNING indicator switches.

When the AOA DISAGREE warning message illuminates, it should be yellow in color and trigger the MASTER CAUTION indicator switches.

Although neither FDR from Preliminary Reports had a trace for the MASTER WARNING indicator, I can assure you it did go off in the cockpit when SPD TRIM FAIL and MACH TRIM FAIL were displayed on the pilot's PFD (if the 737 MAX has one).

Some may find it peculiar that both SPD TRIM FAIL and MACH TRIM FAIL would illuminate when MCAS software takes control, but, MCAS overrides both those software routines in the FCC. Speed Trim controls the horizontal stabilizer and Mach Trim controls the elevators on the horizontal stabilizer. For MCAS to be effective, it has to cease those two other functions in the FCC.

At this point it should be noted that Boeing does not have a message to the pilots when MCAS software is active, it should. In green letters the message displayed needs to be "MCAS" and operate exactly like the message "A/P" occurs on the pilot's PFD when the autopilot is engaged. "MCAS" should be displayed at the top of the PFD's when MCAS is activated. Again, another way the software code was written that failed the pilots.

Probably only software engineers (i.e. programmers) know about a watchdog timer sub-routine; this is one method programmers use to make sure the software is running correctly. A counter is used in a partition like MCAS, and when the software is functioning normally, it resets itself before it is checked by the main program. If a watchdog timer ever counts down to zero, then the next time its checked, the software will stop the subroutine and an error message will be displayed (simplest definition is given – actually much more complex than I describe). In MCAS software, when it fails for any reason, a MCAS FAIL must be displayed.

Boeing's CEO, Dennis Muilenburg, has publicly lied about this AOA DISAGREE warning. He is trying to mislead the general public by saying this warning message is only for maintenance, and that it is not a safety of flight warning, merely advisory. He is using a tactic called the BIG LIE, a propaganda method that relies on the hearer not questioning the statement because they cannot imagine a sane person lying about something so outrageous.

Even the acting F.A.A. Administrator, Daniel K. Elwell, parroted this same lie. Whereas Boeing's CEO lied, he is only an engineer, and Boeing's public relations department may have convinced him to repeat this lie. However, Mr. Elwell was a commercial airlines pilot and **_knows_** that statement is a bold face lie.

This warning message that Boeing's CEO lied about, can only be seen in flight, software does not allow this warning to be displayed on the ground. Maintenance personnel do not fly on an aircraft in the cockpit, unless it is something like a test flight, which the F.A.A. does not allow to happen with any revenue paying passengers aboard.

Maintenance can see the reason the warning message was triggered by going through diagnostic pages on the ground, through the MFD.

QUESTION: WHY DID LION AIR REPLACE THE ORIGINAL AOA SENSOR?

The original AOA sensor may not have been bad. Each of the two Air Data Inertial Reference Units (ADIRU's) are linked to both AOA sensors, the Captain's ADIRU could have an intermittent defective component causing it to send bad data to the MCAS software in the FCC.

Another cause could be something wrong with the 28 VDC power going to the ADIRU's and FCC's.

Overhauled parts are supposed to be equal to new parts, regarding serviceability, although it is not always the case, I've noticed this repeatedly in the years of my long work history. Mechanical defects are going to happen with more frequency than electronic defects, so naturally the AOA sensor that was replaced is the primary suspect.

In my experience working on 737's, AOA sensors often go bad, because they are exposed to the elements and can be physically damaged while the aircraft is sitting on the ramp. There was one instance where I replaced an AOA sensor on a Boeing 737, and then the newly installed sensor did not pass the test after installation, and I ended up having to replace it a second time, the next one passed all of the tests. (I cannot remember if it was a new or overhauled unit; the first AOA sensor I installed had an up angle, consistently of $^+15°$.)

Even back in 2016, the F.A.A. published Airworthiness Directive 2016-25-26 to add heaters to existing AOA sensors, due to failure in icing conditions. AOA sensors are supposed to be environmentally sealed, but due to time and the harsh conditions they operate in, seals can get damaged/worn, and be ineffective, hence the need for heaters at high altitudes. (The higher an aircraft fly's, the colder it gets.)

Although non-experts look at the AOA sensors as providing direct data to the pilots, that is no longer the case in the 737 MAX. In earlier versions of the 737, the two AOA sensors effectively fed mechanical dial gages on the instrument panel, on the left and right side of the instrument panel. Each dial gage was fed by an independent AOA sensor.

On the previous Lion Air flight (JT043), only the night before the crash, a similar malfunction happened to that same airplane. Thankfully for the flight crew flying the 737 MAX 8 that night, an off-duty pilot from Batik Air was onboard the aircraft, seated in the cockpit jump seat. He was able to deactivate the MCAS software by turning off both power switches of STAB TRIM – PRI and B/U, that powered the electric trim system to CUT OUT (OFF), after it started to pitch the aircraft down and the pilots could not initially overcome it manually. Those two switches are located on the pedestal between both pilots, they are on the First Officer's side.

In previous 737's these two STAB TRIM switches were labeled MAIN ELEC and AUTO PILOT. Flipping the left switch to CUT OFF would kill power to the electrical motor driving the horizontal stabilizer. Moving the right switch to CUT OFF would eliminate power to the autopilot (which includes the FCC).[18]

When Boeing engineers created MCAS, they not only renamed both switches, but they changed their function as well. All 737 MAX airplanes have each switch removing power to the electric motor, so now each switch performs the exact same function.[19] In previous versions of the 737, one switch would kill power to the electric motor that moved the jackscrew, the other switch turned off the autopilot system.

QUESTION: WHY CHANGE THE TRIM SWITCH FUNCTION?

If a pilot would move the second switch to CUT OUT, it would disable the autopilot, and in doing so, the FCC inside the 737 MAX would have its power removed as well. Can't fly a 737 MAX without MCAS, so that is the reason the second switch is the same as the other one.

QUESTION: WHAT IS IMPORTANT ABOUT THESE TWO TRIM SWITCHES?

One of the driving forces behind the 737 MAX, is it would require no full flight simulator training.[20] So, Boeing kept both switches to match previous 737 cockpits, and relabeled the switches, now each one performing the exact same task, killing power to the electric motor connected to the jackscrew. Moving the right switch to CUT OFF no longer kills power to the autopilot. (Boeing did not have to re-write any

---

[18] The Seattle Times, "Boeing altered key switches in 737 MAX cockpit, limiting ability to shut off MCAS", Mike Baker and Dominic Gates, 5/10/2019
[19] Boeing (website – http://www.b737.org.uk), Runaway Stabilizer Procedure
[20] The Seattle Times, "Lack of redundancies on Boeing 737 MAX system baffles some involved in developing the jet", Mike Baker and Dominic Gates, 3/26/2019

NON-NORMAL CHECKLISTS because they kept both STAB TRIM switches, but only needed one.)

To understand why a pilot would take such action to kill power to STAB TRIM, a person must know about "Runaway Trim," which occurs when the STAB TRIM motor powers the horizontal stabilizer (small wings located on each side of the tail) into a full nose up or full nose down condition by turning the airplanes' jackscrew until it hits a mechanical stop. A definite way to stop this in previous 737's was to turn both STAB TRIM power switches to the CUT OFF position. In the 737 MAX, turning either of those switches to CUT OFF will kill power to the electric motor.

There are 2 common causes of Runaway Trim: if the elevators are jammed and no longer move, or if the Pitch Trim thumb switches on the pilot's yoke get stuck in either the nose up or nose down position.

(In smaller airplanes a somewhat rarer instance can occur for Runaway Trim, where either of the relays in the electric STAB TRIM system malfunction, delivering the voltage to the electric motor that drives the jackscrew fully up or fully down.)

One likely possibility for taking such action, is the off-duty pilot thought the aircraft had a Runaway Trim situation, and shut off power to the STAB TRIM system, inadvertently turning off the MCAS software's ability to move the horizontal stabilizer. None of the pilots knew anything about MCAS.

However, MCAS commands are quite different from Runaway Trim. MCAS applies a pitch trim signal for 9.26 seconds, then stops and waits for 5 seconds to see if it corrected the AOA problem. Runaway Trim is a constant pitch trim signal (either up or down). **MCAS IS VERY DIFFERENT THAN RUNAWAY TRIM !!!** If either pilot uses Pitch Trim thumb switches on the yoke, that will override MCAS – stopping it, hence it is not Runaway Trim. In a Runaway Trim situation, the Pitch Trim thumb switches have no effect.

After disabling the electrical STAB TRIM system, the horizontal stabilizer can be controlled by a mechanical Pitch Trim Wheel, located by the pilot's knee. In practice, this wheel is very rarely used, mostly because of the force required, and it takes multiple turns to be effective.

Normally, the Pitch Trim thumb switches on both pilot's yokes manually control the horizontal stabilizer. If the STAB TRIM systems fail in flight, then the Pitch Trim Wheel is manually moved to control the horizontal stabilizer using a cable that turns the jackscrew in the tail.

Another factor must be considered here as well. Boeing disabled the pilot's ability to disengage the STAB TRIM system that had been used on all previous 737's without documenting it. Nothing was mentioned by Boeing about disabling the safety features of STAB TRIM, so in the short 56-minute training video given to pilots on their iPads to describe the differences between the 737 MAX 8 and previous 737s, disabling safety mechanisms were not elaborated on. Nor was MCAS described, even briefly, in the 1,400-page Aircraft Flight Manual (AFM) pilots use to understand the aircraft.

All the other previous 737s could have the STAB TRIM system disengaged by a hard pull on the yoke, which is no longer the case in the 737 MAX. One other method was to pull back on the yoke far enough – all the way to mechanical stops. In doing so the Pitch Trim Limit Switches, located by the yoke under the floor; would disable the Pitch Trim system (STAB TRIM). Those Pitch Trim Limit Switches are still physically installed in the 737 MAX but are only used by the Speed Trim system.

I've replaced these Pitch Trim Limit Switches many times. More often than not the wires break at the switch, so a simple repair is common on these switches buried in the cockpit console, or below the floor on some airplanes.

7. ETHIOPIAN AIR FLIGHT ET302

Ethiopian Air Flight ET302 crashed on March 10, 2019 near the town of Bishoftu, Ethiopia. It was scheduled to land at Nairobi, Kenya. The crash killed all 157 people on board. The impact left a crater over 30 feet deep, 90 feet long, and 130 feet wide, just over 30 miles from where it took off. This is the second new 737 MAX 8 aircraft (it was in service only 1,330 flight hours), to crash in 132 calendar days.

Take-off occurred on March 10, 2019, at 8:38 AM local time (05:38:40) UTC, from Addis Ababa Bole International Airport, which is 7,625 feet above sea level. Flight time for ET302 was slightly over 5 minutes from the time it was airborne until the time it crashed.

Horizontal stabilizer pitch was set at 5.6 units, by the pilots before the take-off roll. Engine throttles were set at 94% of maximum power.

	Ethiopian Air Flight ET302 Timeline
05:38:43	• ET302 was at 50 ft. (RALT)
05:38:44	• AOA sensor problem occurs
05:38:45	• Captain's Stick Shaker activates (constant vibration and noise above 85 dB), continues for rest of flight, except near the very end, when it goes off for a few seconds
05:38:46	• **MASTER CAUTION** illuminates (200 ft., RALT), (probably illuminated by AOS sensors disagreeing), pilots push the indicator/switch to turn it off after 9 seconds
05:38:58	• Captain pushes A/P button, Autopilot disconnect tone (400 ft. RALT), autopilot does not engage
05:39:00	• Captain pushes A/P button, Autopilot disconnect tone (630 ft. RALT), autopilot does not engage

05:39:22	• Captain pushes A/P button, Autopilot engages
05:39:25	• Speed Trim (?) gives brief commands to horizontal stabilizer for 30 seconds (until MCAS takes control 35 seconds later)
05:39:46	• Pilot moves flap handle to 0° (fully retracted)
05:39:55	• Autopilot disengages (reason unknown, possibly MCAS) • ET302 is approximately 1,800 above ground level
05:40:00	• MCAS activates and commands *AND*, 2.5 units (moves horizontal stabilizer from 4.6 to 2.1 units) • Both pilots start pulling back on yoke to try and stop MCAS commands, and remain pulling it back until end of the flight, hand flying airplane to end of flight
05:40:03	• GPWS audio warning "DON'T SINK"
05:40:06	• Flaps up (fully retracted)
05:40:20	• MCAS commands *AND* three times, (moves horizontal stabilizer to 0.4 units, near maximum nose down)
05:40:28	• Pilots use Pitch Trim thumbwheel switches to command change the horizontal stabilizer position from 0.4 to 2.3 units of trim
05:40:56	• SIC contacts ATC and tells them that ET302 is having flight control problems • ET302 airspeed 330 knots • ET302 altitude is approximately 3,000 ft. above ground level
05:41:20	• Overspeed audio warning sounds (clacker), continuous until end of flight
05:41:46	• SIC tries to move Pitch Trim Wheel manually, unable to move it
05:42:51	• **MASTER CAUTION** illuminates, "LEFT ALPHA VANE" called out by pilots, they turn

		off LEFT AOA HEAT seconds later
05:43:10	•	Pilots use Pitch Trim thumbwheel switches to give nose up command (airplane does not respond)
	•	ET302 altitude is approximately 6,000 ft. above ground level
05:43:14	•	Pilots use Pitch Trim thumbwheel switches to give another nose up command (airplane does not respond)
05:43:15	•	Captain pushes A/P button, Autopilot disconnect tone, autopilot does not engage
05:43:25	•	MCAS gives its 4th *AND* command, putting the airplane into a dive
05:43:27	•	All passengers have 0 "g's" of force on them (they feel weightless)
05:43:43	•	ET302 impacts Earth

Soon after the stick shaker first went off, the First Officer failed to call-out the mandatory items like SPEED, etc. It is my opinion the lack of call-outs was more due to the noise level created by the Stick Shaker, the First Officer would have to yell to be heard over that background noise, contributing to the stress the Captain was already dealing with.

After the autopilot is disconnected, GPWS issues "DON'T-SINK, DON'T-SINK" warnings at least 4 separate times, through the cockpit speaker.

It must be emphasized that ET302 and JT610 were dissimilar when thinking about passengers in the cabin compartment. <u>The flight crew in JT610 was fighting MCAS and everyone in the cabin felt like they were on a bad rollercoaster ride.</u> Yet, although the flight crew of ET302 also fought with MCAS, passengers felt like they were in heavy turbulence. ET302 went up and down quickly, whereas the people in JT610 the ups and downs were more gradual, but each of those highs and lows were really extreme.

Airspeed steadily increases slowly for the whole flight, until the aircraft speed is near 500 knots, in a near straight-down vertical dive for an airplane. (Airplanes typically land at a 3° down angle, the aircraft crashed at over a 40° down angle.)

Quite few things were happening, besides having the pilots fight MCAS commands.

Looking at a crude paper graph of the FDR data, provided in the Preliminary Report by the Ethiopian Ministry of Transport, the aircraft did more than just change direction.

At 05:42:25 (UTC) in the flight, the aircraft rolled 15°, and at 05:43:25 it rolled even further to 30°.

I've flown as part of F.A.A. Flight Check missions, and in one required maneuver the airplane would roll left and then immediately roll right (+/- 20°). Pretty impressive, I still remember it 30 years later. In this flight they experience very rough turbulence, and steep banks of the airplane occurred as well.

One thing that stood out to me was that at the end of flight ET302 the pilots used the Pitch Trim thumbwheel switches, with NO effect.

If anyone examined the FDR data and became puzzled at why the pilots didn't use the Pitch Trim thumbwheel switches more often, that's why. There was too much of a lag time between moving those switches and that movement actually being processed in the FCC, then being finally sent as drive commands to the electric motor attached to the jackscrew. Pilots of ET302 were not just in a tussle with MCAS, but the pitch response time was too slow, the only tool the flight crew had to counter those MCAS pitch down commands (**AND**) took too long to work.

The pilots did call out "**MASTER CAUTION – LEFT ALPHA VANE**" though. It is not of vital interest that the First Officer did his duty on calling out a safety of flight item, what is important is why he called it out.

LEFT ALPHA VANE is related to the anti-icing circuitry of the Captain's AOA sensor. Both the **MASTER CAUTION** and the call-out happened at 05:42:51 UTC. Either it was an internal malfunction (which I suspect), or a bird strike that not only sheared off the external portion but internally damaged it (another possibility, but remote in my opinion). Pilots then switched off the LEFT AOA HEAT switch, to prevent a fire.

MCAS executes 3 *AND* (automatic nose down) commands, the pilots counter with two *ANU* (automatic nose up) commands which moves the horizontal stabilizer to 2.4 units at 05:40:28. It is at that time I believe the pilots were following the Airworthiness Directive written directions from the F.A.A., because MCAS does not make any more *AND* commands to the horizontal stabilizer until 05:43:22.

During this time interval of about 3 minutes, the First Officer tried unsuccessfully to move the horizontal stabilizer by hand, using the Pitch Trim Wheel; then the flight crew then turned back on power to the STAB TRIM system so it would be possible to move the horizontal stabilizer using the Pitch Trim thumb switches. After two brief attempts commanding nose up using the Pitch Trim thumb switches with zero results, they didn't use them again.

Then MCAS gives another short *AND* command at 05:43:22 which pitches the nose down again. The pilots keep using the yoke to counteract the commanded dive from MCAS until the airflow is too great on the elevators, it overcomes the power of the hydraulic actuators and forces them into a neutral position (elevator blowback).

At that point the aircraft is sent into an uncontrollable dive, and the crash occurs 5 minutes after lift-off, at 05:43:45.

The horror of 157 human beings who were just like me, dying suddenly at the same place and time – due to poor vehicle design, is hard to comprehend. I write this to prevent a third crash.

If it happens again – shame on us.

People have speculated that the Captain's left (pilot) AOA sensor was damaged by a bird strike a few seconds after take-off. In my analysis of the preliminary FDR data in a paper graph format provided by Ethiopian officials, it is a lot more complicated than that.

Governmental authorities have been provided detailed data from Aireon, this company provides ADS-B coverage from their global satellite network. Every aircraft that is equipped with ADS-B reports to this company a complete list of data points every 8 seconds while airborne.[21] Because of the accurate data Aireon provided, China and the rest of the world (except the F.A.A.) were able to ground the 737 MAX before waiting for the FDR to be recovered and analyzed from flight ET302.

As part of my early avionics career, I had to analyze FDR recordings scribed by movable arms onto metal foil, before the invention of digital recording, and yes, I'm old. Those early devices only recorded 7 parameters. My job was to uncoil the metal tape and check the last flight at the end of each week and see if the FDR recorded it OK and replace the metal foil as necessary (sending the completed roll for analysis).

In the Preliminary Report, they included rude graphs of the important parameters of the FDR, including the AOA sensors. If a

---

[21] Aviation Today, "Global ADS-B Surveillance is Now Live", Nick Zazulia, 4/2/2019

person only looks at the first part of the trace recording, they of course jump to the conclusion of a bird strike. But when analyzing the whole trace, that is an inaccurate description of what happened. The left AOA vane acted almost normal at the end, moments before the crash, most likely invalidating the theory of a bird strike (but would support the theory of an intermittent component inside the FCC).

Human Factors, a very important term used in aviation, describes how humans can be affected by many things. One study into human behavior found that a human's ability to do creative problem-solving decreases by 50% when under stress. (An example of this would be the stick shaker going off consistently without the pilots able to stop the physical vibration or its loud noise above 85 db.)

Taking a class in how to measure sound levels, I was exposed to the concept that not all noise is the same. White noise sounds like a hissing sound, Harley Motorcycles also have a distinct sound. Being exposed to the Sticker Shaker going off in multiple aircraft on the ground, it is not only annoying, but really uncomfortable.

This flight crew was deluged with so many things happening at once, and to the last moment they kept their composure, and tried everything to save their passengers, they performed in real life like the consummate pilots portrayed by Hollywood actors in movies. They may have not been perfect, but they are real heroes to me. It was the plane, its poor design, and incomplete F.A.A. directions, that failed them.

Boeing is blaming both flight crews of pilot error, trying to limit their exposure in +30 lawsuits already filed. Insisting that a chain of events occurred,[22] and that pilot error was the most consequential factor. Nothing could be further from the truth.

---

[22] Washington Post, "FAA chief pilot says pilot decisions contributed to Boeing 737 Max crashes", Micheal Laris, Lori Aratani and Ashley Halsey III, 5/15/2019

Trying to blame the flight crews for both crashes, U.S. pilots look at foreign pilots not being trained enough, and thereby are not qualified to help command a commercial airplane. Both U.S. and foreign countries mandate a minimum of 1,500 flight hours before an individual can be a Captain (PIC). However, countries outside of the U.S. only require 240 hours of flight time for a First Officer (SIC).[23] The 25-year-old SIC had only 360 flight hours before the crash that took his life, but some of those hours were in a 737 MAX 8 simulator.

Adding to the misinformation campaign was Congressman Sam Graves of Missouri (R), at a House Committee hearing on 5/15/2019. Representative Graves parroted the same information Boeing is trying to peddle about pilot error being the most important link in the chain that caused the crash.[24]

Republicans in Congress and officials at Boeing are basing their statements on a report by 2 airline pilots, Don McGregor and Vaughn Cordle. These 2 men investigated both 737 MAX 8 crashes, funded by institutional investors who have a very large number of shares in Boeing stock.[25] (Does anyone else think the conclusions in their investigation were preordained?)

Not to make too fine a point on this, but all 737 NG simulators at the time of their "investigation" could not duplicate MCAS software in the cockpit[26], so how did they arrive at their conclusion it was pilot error? In fact, Boeing has updated the 737 NG flight simulator twice, because it did not accurately represent the force applied to the Pitch Trim Wheels.[27]

---

[23] USA Today, "Boeing 737 Max crash: Did pilots have enough flight training to fly commercial jets?", Chris Woodyard, 7/6/2019

[24] Washington Post, "After two faulty Boeing jets crash, the Trump administration blames foreign pilots, Dana Milbank, 5/16/2019

[25] The Seattle Times, "Ethiopian Airlines calls criticism of its pilots an effort to 'divert public attention' from Boeing 737 MAX flaws", Dominic Gates, 5/17/2019

[26] AFP, "Boeing acknowledges flaw in 737 MAX simulator software" Luc Olinga, 5/20/2019

The pilot's "investigative" report was given to the institutional investors. I would ask how Boeing and Republican Congressmen Sam Graves obtained the report, but being quite old, I do know how the world works. (Money)

QUESTION: DID BOTH FLIGHT CREWS DO EVERYTHING RIGHT?

Simply put, the answer is NO.

Both flight crews exceeded the redline airspeed of the 737 MAX airframe. Only the flight crew of Indonesia Air (JT610) retarded the throttles before the crash, but they were in the air for twice as long... and still died. I must point out an obvious fact; pulling back (retarding) the throttles cause the aircraft to severely pitch down – the very condition both flight crews were fighting, so close to the Earth.

In neither case was Runaway Trim evident, so using that procedure should not have been considered. From a pilot perspective it was not Runaway Trim because pitching down of the airplane was temporary, reversible with thumb switches on the yoke, so they did not understand whether the horizontal stabilizer was the problem or were the elevators the source? (At the end of both flights, the yoke functioned but the elevators did not.)

Blaming the flight crews is something else the F.A.A. has in common with Boeing. They are insisting that the Ethiopian pilots did not follow the Airworthiness Directive (AD) they put out on the 737 MAX.

I've read the AD; it is vague on the procedure to use before turning off both STAB TRIM power switches on the console. No clear language is used to say that before turning off electrical power to the

---

[27] Bloomberg, "Fight for Survival on Doomed Jet Came down to two Cockpit Wheels" Alan Levin, 6/20/2019

STAB TRIM system, first use the Pitch Trim thumb switches on the yoke to obtain straight and level flight BEFORE removing power. Because if the airplane has even a slightly mis-trimmed horizontal stabilizer, you cannot move the Pitch Trim wheel to correct it above 250 knots (IAS) on the 737 MAX.

Interestingly enough, it is my understanding a separate investigation is being conducted by the F.A.A. into all of the 737 airplanes in service; seems every 737 airplane has this "feature" where the Pitch Trim Wheel is too hard physically to move it at high speeds.[28]

Let me redirect the reader to Boeing's claim that a chain of events caused the crash. On that statement I agree… it just wasn't a chain of events inside the cockpit. A chain of small human errors began and ended with Boeing manufacturing the 737 MAX.

Trying to win a competition with Airbus forced the design team into a series of measures helping their team meet schedule deadlines but had disastrous future implications. Now add to that the F.A.A. did not properly oversee the certification process, allowing Boeing to misclassify a flight control system (MCAS software) to be "hazardous". Another link in the chain condemning 346 lives was that Boeing did not put onto paper that it installed a new safety of flight system, anywhere in the pilot manuals.

Pilots flying the 737 MAX had no idea a new flight control system, that could kill them and their passengers was even installed.

Least, but not last, Collins Aerospace wrote the MCAS software, not following Boeing's written software requirements, so there was no **AOA DISAGREE** warning available in 80% of the delivered aircraft. Whomever Boeing employed as their Business Analysts overseeing the software process, did not catch this major problem in software. Boeing

---

[28] Bloomberg, "Fight for Survival on Doomed Jet Came Down to Two Cockpit Wheels", Alan Levin, 6/20/2019

engineers discovered it after the first 737 MAX aircraft were delivered in 2017.

Two Boeing panels/committees concurred this lack of an AOA DISAGREE safety warning was not significant to ground the fleet of 737 MAX airplanes. Compounding this failure, the F.A.A. arrived at the same conclusion, days before the second crash. (6 weeks after the second 737 MAX crash the acting F.A.A. Administrator read about a lack of a safety warning in the newspaper[29] – no one in his organization thought it important enough to inform senior leadership about the lack of a safety warning not displayed to flight crews who died in separate crashes.)

THINK ABOUT IT:

Where did the chain of events occur? Inside or outside of the cockpit?

---

[29] Wall Street Journal, "Boeing Knew About Safety-Alert Problem for a Year Before Telling FAA, Airlines", Andy Pasztor, Andrew Tangel and Alison Sider, 5/5/2019

8. WHY MCAS?

It's complicated.

To create the 737 MAX with larger engines and an airplane design that is prone to aircraft stall, Boeing first removed the Stall Management / Yaw Damper (SMYD) Computers that used to warn pilots of an impending stall. (I'm not smart enough to make this up.) Besides alerting the pilots of a stall, these 2 SMYD computers also had the Elevator Feel Computer (EFC) exert 4 times the necessary effort to pull back the yoke to have the aircraft go nose up; they even had a Radio Altimeter (RALT) input, so it would not activate when too close to the ground.

Instead Boeing added hardware to the 2 existing Flight Control Computers (FCC's), plus a partition in software to house the added MCAS software.

At this point it is imperative to inform anyone who reads this, that the stall warning message only works on 20% of the original 737 MAX fleet, probably due to rushed software coding by Collins Aerospace (manufacturer of the FCC's). Of course, it is just as plausible that Collins used $9 an hour contractors in India to write their software code who had no clue about aviation. On the other hand, Boeing did employ foreign contractors at $9 an hour and they developed the software used to test the 737 MAX airplane for certification.

Boeing has also a R & D (Research and Development) center in Russia.[30] Although not related to the 737 Max, it is indicative of problems encountered when outsourcing to foreign firms who don't have a strong aircraft background. In 2008 one Boeing employee complained to senior management they had to send 787 drawings back

---

[30] Bloomberg, "Boeing's 737 Max software outsorced to $9-an-hour engineers" Peter Robison,

18 times before Russian developers understood a basic concept. *The item in question was smoke detectors.* Russians could not comprehend that smoke detectors in airplanes needed to be connected to the airplane's electrical system. In a person's home, smoke detectors are not normally connected to the electrical house wiring. Unbelievable, but true (it took 18 tries to get it right).

Let me explain MCAS as simply as I can – it's software.

> **QUESTION: WHAT ARE THE PHYSICAL ESSENTIALS OF MCAS SOFTWARE?**

Both FCC's house multiple software functions, besides MCAS. Mach Trim is a system that resides within the FCC and is active at higher airplane speeds. Another separate software function within the FCC is the Speed Trim system which is active at slower airplane speeds.

Looking at MCAS, it is simply software that has been partitioned from other software in the FCC, it is not a stand-alone system. All FCC inputs are already part of the previous 737 model, as are its outputs. Boeing did move the AOA sensor outputs so they could be wired as inputs to both FCC's (probably one AOA fed ADIRU #1 and communicated its data to FCC #1, the other AOA sensor fed ADIRU #2 and it also fed digital data to FCC #2).

Whoever approved MCAS software at Boeing must have looked at it like it was just added functionality to the FCC. They must have thought:
- No need to tell the Test Pilots about it.
- No need to add it to the Aircraft Flight Manual or any other airplane documentation.
- Doing any real-world tests should not include any failure scenarios because MCAS software is already relying on existing hardware.

Even Boeing's CEO, Dennis Muilenburg has publicly stated that MCAS is not a separate system to be trained on."[31]

Of course, I disagree with Boeing focusing attention on MCAS as comprised solely of software inside the FCC. One Boeing executive flippantly said that MCAS software is just "several lines of code" to make all 737's *feel* the same to the pilots.

Boeing had designed an unstable aircraft and needed flight-by-wire controls to keep the 737 MAX from pitching nose up in flight, stalling, and crashing the airplane due to design errors in the pitch axis. For the entire system to work correctly Boeing had to remove total control from the pilots. (Such autonomy, with no limits, needed to have been tested for all failure modes, and someone at Boeing needed to classify MCAS software as a safety of flight *critical* system, requiring redundancy.)

Both FCC's (Captain and First Officer – #1 and #2) have this software partition for MCAS. MCAS is in both FCC's, yet Boeing did not take the time to make this a redundant system. Each AOA sensor feeds one of the FCC's, the left goes into the Captains side (#1), the right AOA sensor is input into the First Officer's side (#2). Whichever FCC is active will use its own AOA sensor.

There are reasons why both FCC's are identical. Technicians need to be able to swap the #1 (Captain's) with the #2 (First Officer's) for troubleshooting purposes. Logistically, both need to be the same for fewer spares needing to be stored on a parts shelf, as a single unit costs $200,000.

When Airbus designed their first iteration of the A320, it was a fly-by-wire aircraft. The wings were placed high enough to mount a CFM LEAP 1A jet engine on without having to use additional electronics like

---

[31] Business Insider, "Boeing's CEO explains why the company didn't tell 737 MAX pilots about the software system that contributed to 2 fatal crashes", Benjamin Zhang, 4/30/2019

the 737 MAX does with MCAS. Instead of a standard yoke to control flight surfaces, each pilot has a joystick in the A320.

Military stealth aircraft are inherently unstable in flight, whereas a human cannot possibly fly them without computer assistance; for the most part, all these new military designs since 1980, have incorporated fly-by-wire.

A dynamically unstable aircraft will use the fly-by-wire computers to compensate for all the variables that are encountered in flight for an unstable aircraft, making it safe to fly.

Aerodynamics of the 737 MAX in computer modelling and wind tunnel testing back in 2012 revealed the aircraft tends to pitch up its nose, because Center of Gravity (CG) and Center of Lift (CL) are too close together. These two, CG and CL, are so near each other because of the new engine placement.

Wind tunnel testing is used to simulate actual flight situations while using a scaled down model of the airplane to be manufactured. One critical objective the 737 MAX failed in was longitudinal stability, specifically it failed in the "Windup Turn".[32] [33] Specific requirements for this type of flight testing can be found in 14 CFR 25.255.

There is a reason why a Windup Turn is so critical for a commercial airliner, it simulates the conditions where an airplane must avoid an obstacle (airplane, or wind vortex) at cruise speed and altitude. If a 747 wide body airplane was to have an emergency – lose altitude and suddenly appear in front of the 737 MAX flight path, then this maneuver would have to be performed, while not endangering the passengers; it can cause forces of up to 3 "g's" to be felt inside the 737 MAX.

---

[32] The Seattle Times, "The inside story of MCAS: How Boeing's 737 MAX system gained power and lost safeguards" Dominic Gates and Mike Baker, 6/22/2019
[33] NASA, Information Summaries, IS-97/08-DFRC-WUT, Windup Turn

In 2012, Ray Craig (Boeing's Chief Test Pilot at that time) noticed this failure in the simulator.[34]

Windup Turns are used to check stability at high angles of attack, while at cruise power and at higher altitudes. Basically, the aircraft is at cruise altitude and speed when the simulator pilot makes a coordinated turn. Without advancing engine power, he/she must maintain a constant speed – by pitching down the aircraft. Fighter aircraft are highly unstable and finish this same maneuver at 7 "g's" and are in a near vertical dive. An F-18 fighter jet has an instability factor of 5%,[35] whereas the 737 MAX unstableness factor is below 1%, but still sufficient enough to cause it to crash. No other commercial airplane flying passengers is unstable.

When simulator pilots pulled back on the yoke of the 737 MAX in the coordinated turn (Windup Turn), it was not a smooth and continuous feel on the yoke, there were periods where the yoke felt slack while turning.

To prevent failing this flight critical test on the 737 MAX, engineers invented MCAS. Initially only 0.6 units of horizontal stabilizer trim were required to pass this test.

MCAS was designed for high speeds when an aircraft approaches Mach 1, the speed of sound. At higher Mach numbers, such as above Mach 0.5 the airplane starts to lose lift as its speed increases while reducing the AOA value it will stall at. Now imagine the unstable 737 MAX trying to perform a high-speed turn, and then you will understand why MCAS is desperately needed (cannot be flown without it).

---

[34] New York Times, "Boeing Built Deadly Assumptions Into 737 MAX, Blind to a Late Design Change", Jack Nicas, Natalie Kitroef, David Gelles, and James Glanz, 6/1/2019

[35] CNN, "Grumman X-29: The impossible fighter jet with inverted wings. Experimental design aerodynamically unstable", Jacopo Prisco, 7/14/2019

Actual flight testing of the proto-type aircraft determined this was even more significant in real life.

Typically, a 737 MAX 8 can fly at Mach 0.78 (520 knots, 598 mph) at cruise altitudes. Also, the weight upon take-off can exceed 180,000 pounds. Now imagine that heavy gigantic aircraft losing lift, hurtling at those speeds... nose up... dropping like a stone – tail first.

To help you comprehend how big the 737 MAX really is, think of an empty railroad freight car, its 50 ft. long and weighs 60,000 lbs. Three of these freight cars equal the length of a 737 MAX and weigh as much as one fully loaded. If 3 of those boxcars could be welded together, then use your imagination and envision them being towed by a 747 going 600 mph using a big rope at 35,000 ft. in altitude. Now, cut the rope.

Let me reiterate, Boeing's initial fix to the 737 MAX is to turn off MCAS when the pair of AOA sensors disagree by 5.5°, which will cause a disaster if that occurs and an airplane needs to perform a Windup Turn maneuver to avoid an obstacle while cruising at altitude. Maybe, chances of that happening could occur once every 5,000,000 flight hours, but very plausible, knowing how unreliable AOA sensors are. How are the pilots going to recover from that scenario? They won't recover. Stall must be avoided!

Compare the above with a Cessna 172, weighing just over 2,400 lbs., traveling at 110 knots. Putting the nose down to gain airspeed and lift would be a simple thing after encountering a stall condition.

The Cessna 172 is a very aerodynamically stable aircraft. So much so that if a pilot was at a high enough altitude, he/she could let go of the yoke, and the airplane would eventually center itself.

Boeing invented MCAS software to prevent a stall condition from ever happening in the 737 MAX.

> QUESTION: WHY DID THEY NEED TO MODIFY A 737, AND NOT START ON A NEW DESIGN?

Airbus started in late 2010, designing a refresh of their A320 aircraft; putting efficient engines onto the existing airframe, thereby saving 15% in fuel costs, and calling it A320NEO (New Engine Option). Airbus uses CFM's LEAP 1A jet engines on the A320, whereas the 737MAX 8 uses the CFM LEAP 1B jet engines. **Airbus has no trouble with the same engine design.**

In 2010, Boeing was still considering a clean-sheet type of aircraft, a completely new design, to replace the 737 which could take a decade or more.

Airbus announced its intention to modify its existing A320 aircraft with fuel efficient engines (LEAP 1A) at the end of 2010. About 6 months later, at the Paris Air Show of 2011, Airbus presold 667 A320NEO's in one week. Currently Airbus has more than 6,000 backordered A320NEO airplanes, compared to the 5,000 Boeing's 737 MAX on order.

To keep up, Boeing decided in August 2011, to use its existing 737 airframe, that was first flown in 1967, to accelerate the design process, so it could keep up with its only real competitor, Airbus. (Its rumored that what changed Boeing's decision was when American Airline's CEO spoke with Boeing's CEO about switching to the Airbus A320NEO, to save fuel costs, not waiting for a new aircraft from Boeing, back in June of 2011.)

After discussing this with the rest of the Boeing's Board of Directors, the Chairman/CEO made the decision to develop the 737 MAX aircraft in August 2011, putting Boeing nine months behind Airbus, in their race to sell a new fuel-efficient aircraft.

A major problem using the ancient existing design of the 737 from the 1960's, was when the original was created, there were no jetways at the airports. All passengers left the terminal, climbed the stairs integral to the front aircraft door, and then they boarded onto the 737.

The 737 was designed to be low to the ground for passenger loading and unloading. Baggage handlers did not need a conveyer belt, maintenance personnel could service the engines faster, not needing ladder stands for routine tasks.

Engine placement was dictated to be under the wing, to reduce load on the fuselage; doing this there would be 3 seats on each side of the aisle of the 737. Eventually this killed off one of their competitors, the Douglas DC-9, because it only had a total of 5 passenger seats across each aisle.

Back then, most commercial aircraft had 3 members of the flight crew in the commercial jet cockpits. Boeing designed the original 737 to only need 2 pilots as a flight crew. Another way Boeing could steal market share. (As Boeing is designing the new 797, they are considering a single pilot on board, a second pilot will be on the ground responsible for 9 other airplanes as well.)

The die was cast way back in 2004, for the tragedy to occur almost 15 years later. Congress had the F.A.A. appear before them on Capitol Hill, trying to determine if deregulation was good, of course the F.A.A. agreed, because it would save the agency money.

Eventually the F.A.A. created a system where large aircraft manufacturers would inspect themselves, with a handful of F.A.A. Airworthiness Safety Inspectors (ASI's) overseeing the company's inspectors. Almost all the Manufacturing ASI's employed by the F.A.A. retired or transferred to other positions, there are a total of just 18 Manufacturing Inspection District Offices (MIDO's) in the U.S. today. An Organization Designation Authorization (ODA) program was created in 2005, letting the F.A.A. designate inspectors to inspect the company they work for; it went live in 2009. After 2 years, companies named their own inspectors, without F.A.A. input.

Currently Boeing has approximately 950 F.A.A. designated manufacturing inspectors, called Authorized Representatives (AR's), for a workforce of 130,000 employees, paid by Boeing.

Engineers comprise almost 40% of Boeing's workforce, scattered across the country. In a strictly paperwork oversight capacity, the F.A.A. has about 25 ASI's overseeing Boeing. Think of all the money the government has been able to redirect (because the government never saves, nor asks for less, government only spends it somewhere else).

Fast forward from 2004 to 2011 when the 737 MAX was conceived, there was huge political pressure to save good paying union jobs, just like the ones Boeing had. America was recovering from the recession that started in 2008. Bailout of the auto industry was underway. Unemployment was soaring.

If Boeing did not compete with Airbus, it would be catastrophic economically. Boeing is the largest exporter in America, it accounts for more than 0.2% of U.S. GDP. Losing a decade of aircraft sales to Airbus while Boeing did a ground up new aircraft design, would probably make them face bankruptcy. Taking a broad, sky-high view of the 2011 economy: a stock market crisis was already occurring, what if Boeing and all 900 suppliers went into the toilet? These are the issues politicians were looking at in 2011. And Politicians of all types put pressure on the F.A.A. to save jobs in their district, Boeing having disbursed its 900 suppliers to all over the country. Pressure which in turn went from F.A.A. headquarters, to managers in all their field offices.

In this climate, you can now understand why the F.A.A. felt pressure from politics to green light the 737 MAX design. Add to that the fact they no longer physically inspected the manufacturing process, Boeing seemed to have cut corners to jump start their 737 MAX design to keep up with the A320NEO – a recipe for disaster.

Today, all airplane manufacturers look like they are in a race to the bottom. Not one appears to be doing anything beyond the minimum requirements, even the F.A.A. has been cited for performing only the minimum inspection requirements. Airlines are trying to offer cheaper plane tickets, so naturally they look for the cheapest deal on the planes they purchase.

When I mention cutting corners, it is not shoddy work or suspected materials they are using. No, I'm specifically talking about Boeing's managers, their performance appraisals were based in part on if they met scheduled deadlines and were able to reduce costs. In turn, this related to managers insisting compliant engineers get testing done in a shortened time frame and at minimal costs.

Why else do you think Boeing never tested an AOA sensor failure in flight testing of MCAS software? Failure of an AOA sensor was only analyzed in design and certification, never tested on a stationary flight simulator, like the one Boeing owns in Seattle, Washington.[36]

Add to that the "FAA Reauthorization Act of 2018" signed into law, weeks before the first 737 MAX 8 crash. Inside this new law, the F.A.A. is required to "delegate fully" unless the F.A.A. Administrator (or designee) determines there is a specific reason to revoke any portion of the ODA.[37] In the case where some portion of an ODA is revoked, the F.A.A. Administrator (or designee) **MUST** work with the manufacturer to get the full ODA back.

Entrenched in Congress is the mindset to minimize government cost, shifting the burden unto others. Government passing inspection costs onto business does not just apply to aviation, but mining, food inspection and other similar functions are being forced into self-inspection.

---

[36] CNN, "Boeing relied on single sensor for 737 Max that had been flagged 216 times to FAA", Curt Devine and Drew Griffin, 4/30/2019

[37] The Seattle Times, "With close industry ties, FAA safety chief pushed more delegation of oversight to Boeing", Dominic Gates, 4/14/2019

Rockwell Collins (now its name has been changed to Collins Aerospace, after United Technologies acquired them in 2018) was tapped to write the software for MCAS, as well as design the hardware to run it. Previously they won the contract to do the same thing for Boeing on their Flight Control Computers (FCC's) in 2003, which they now sell back to Boeing at $200,000 a pop; each 737 has 2 FCC's.[38]

To fully automate MCAS, Boeing engineers removed all of the things that could disable STAB TRIM in the previous 737 models, without telling anyone. (Although the Pitch Trim Limit Switches are still physically there, MCAS software simply disregards them.)

Because of a lack of oversight, Boeing engineers considered high speed cruise would be the only condition MCAS would be needed to prevent stall. Envisioning a scenario where the aircraft was at high speed cruise, where the flight crew had to turn the airplane in a radical turn, MCAS would intervene and prevent a stall of the 737 MAX.

THINK ABOUT IT:

What were the reasons they never considered take-off?

Were there no 737 test-pilots part of their final discussions?

---

[38] The Washington Post, "Boeing's 737 Max design contains fingerprints of hundreds of suppliers", Douglas MacMillan and Aaron Gregg, 4/5/2019

9. WHAT DOES MCAS ACTUALLY DO?

Design of the 737 MAX is different aerodynamically from all other 737 models, so MCAS software is only installed in it.

Collins Aerospace makes the Flight Control Computer (FCC), the hardware inside it, along with creating the coding of the MCAS software that runs inside both FCC's.[39]

Originally MCAS software was supposed to have inputs from an AOA sensor (angle of the wind outside the fuselage of the 737 MAX), and a vertical acceleration sensor (vertical "g" force) from an Air Data Inertial Reference Unit (ADIRU).

Ed Wilson, chief test pilot for Boeing on the 737 MAX, after Ray Craig left, sensed it didn't handle low speed stalls very well and told this to the engineering staff; he thought the yoke did not feel smooth near low speed stall.[40] To make MCAS effective at slower speeds, Boeing engineers removed the vertical acceleration input, and effectively changed the Speed Trim system to let MCAS have authority outside of its intended scope.

At lower speeds the 737 MAX would need more than 0.6 units of trim to be effective, so Boeing engineered MCAS to have 2.5 units of command authority over the horizontal stabilizer. Then, not only MCAS would fire once, but activate consecutively after a 5 second waiting period, if it determined the 737 MAX was still approaching a stall. And if that was not bad enough, they engineered the MCAS

---

[39] The Washington Post, "Boeing's 737 Max design contains fingerprints of hundreds of suppliers", Douglas MacMillan and Aaron Gregg, 4/5/2019

[40] New York Times, "Boeing Built Deadly Assumptions Into 737 MAX, Blind to a Late Design Change", Jack Nicas, Natalie Kitroef, David Gelles, and James Glanz, 6/1/2019

software to be reset, and fire off a 2.5 unit command after either pilot moved the Pitch Trim thumb switches on the yoke.

> **QUESTION: WHY DIDN'T BOEING HAVE MCAS WORK ON A GRADUAL SLIDING SCALE?**

At slower speeds MCAS software needed to command 2.5° trim every 10 seconds. Only about 0.6° trim was required at higher speeds. It appears Boeing choose 2.5° trim units for all MCAS software activations. What adjective would I use for this, picking a single value to apply to all speeds? Lazy, Incompetent, Reckless, ??? (select one)

Every 737 MAX has 2 FCC units, each has the MCAS software inside it. Yet MCAS has no redundancy, for a safety of flight mission critical system; only one FCC is active each flight. It's hard to imagine why the 737 MAX, having 2 AOA sensors, and 2 FCC's, chose not to make MCAS a redundant system. (Again, another area to examine, when prosecuting attorneys are considering criminal negligence charges. Plus, any cover-up of these decisions or deleting/trashing associated documents would be another crime as well, which is currently being investigated by the Department of Justice, Fraud Division.)

I have examined rough graphs from 3 different flights where MCAS 100% activated in, the following are my observations.

Actual implementation of MCAS software is supposed to act when:
1. AOA sensor detects a stall (YES)*
2. Weight on Wheels indicates airplane is airborne (YES) *
3. Exceeds speed of 225 knots (above 180 knots at low altitude) *
4. Autopilot not engaged (MCAS will disengage autopilot before it acts) *
5. Flaps are fully retracted (YES)*
    * (observed from FDR graphs)

Like making sausage, this process becomes ugly once its examined.

Boeing, having removed the SMYD computers, the FCC now controls the stick shaker mounted on the pilot's yoke; it is independent from MCAS.

If the autopilot is engaged when the FCC decides that the 737 MAX is approaching a stall, it will disengage the autopilot automatically, plus prevent the autopilot from reengaging while MCAS is active.

Another point for Regulatory Agency investigators to look at is the fact that MCAS is required for flight. Are the appropriate systems reflected in the Minimum Equipment List, since all systems feeding MCAS must be active and airworthy before a 737 MAX can be dispatched for scheduled flight operations? What I'm hinting at is many parts of the autopilot system can be inoperative, but nothing that MCAS needs to work can be inoperative if the 737 MAX wants to fly.

A lot of what MCAS software can do is described in the previous chapters.

My personal disclaimer, I don't have hands-on experience with the 737 MAX aircraft. My experience is with prior 737 models, along with the A320NEO, and many other commercial aircraft. I'm not an aircraft pilot.

Detailing exactly how MCAS functions is very important to connect the dots on why both aircraft crashed.

Before a discussion of how MCAS software caused 2 aircraft to crash on take-off, a person should understand how a 737 MAX achieves take-off.

Departing from a major airport that has air carrier service (airlines), commercial pilots normally use Standard Instrument Departure (SID) procedures, developed by F.A.A. procedures pilots or contractors.

Every airport runway departure procedure will state a minimum climb rate, but, if an aircraft can climb faster, it is allowed.

Boeing 737's pilots typically set their climb at an angle between 3.0 units and 8.0 units (as indicated on the control column, located next to the Pitch Trim Wheel) for take-off in most circumstances. Field elevation, barometric altimeter reading, weight, temperature, fuel load, and other factors can affect the climb rate. Pushing the throttles to take-off power also adds a lot of pitch to the aircraft (as the thrust increases, so does airplane pitch = physics).

As an Avionics Technician I approach this subject a little differently, although what the pilot sees, and how the aircraft behaves – correlates; yet I know different.

Typically, the maximum travel of the horizontal stabilizer is physically 4.2° leading edge up (nose down ↓) and 12.9° leading edge down (nose up ↑). Although this is shown on the control column as 0 units to 17 units. (0 units = full nose down, 17 units = full nose up), anyone can see units of trim do not directly associate with degrees of elevation of the horizontal stabilizer.

Yet, one unit of trim shown on the control column equals 1.0° of horizontal movement.

A reading of 0 units indicated on the control column is FULL NOSE DOWN of the horizontal stabilizer. This is of vital importance to understanding how both crashes occurred. Not to get lost in the nuts and bolts of tech speak, MCAS has only to cycle 2 times to force the aircraft into a FULL DOWN nosedive (if it is reset by either Pitch Trim thumb switch).

A loosely applied rule by the F.A.A. is to have aircraft below 10,000 ft. in altitude, not to exceed 250 knots per hour. (If an aircraft has a valid reason for exceeding this speed limit in the sky, they can.)

Once a commercial pilot reaches Vr (speed at which they can pull up on the yoke and go "wheels up" = Velocity for rotation) on the runway, they typically climb fast, their throttles are at a near maximum position. They retract flaps and landing gear almost immediately when they get into the air.

For a 737 to accelerate to Vr speed on the runway, throttles are set to "take-off" position (pretty much full throttle). Pilots do not retard the throttles until they achieve V2 (speed in which it is safe to maneuver the aircraft), that takes a few moments after take-off.

Take-off is the worst flight profile for the 737 MAX, when it is the most unstable, exactly a condition MCAS software was designed for, but I don't think Boeing engineers anticipated it would actually activate while in a take-off profile.

Once MCAS software determines it is to engage, it initially forces the horizontal stabilizer into 2.5 units pitch down, incrementally afterwards it commands 0.5 units, moving the entire horizontal stabilizer up (large surface), forcing the aircraft to pitch down. *Physics dictate that to get out of a stall, point the aircraft nose down, increasing speed, which increases airflow over the wings, thereby increasing lift.*

On take-off, throttles are at near maximum making the aircraft exceed 230 knots, once airborne, flaps are retracted, and the landing gear is up, satisfying all of the conditions for MCAS. Once it senses a stall for any reason if its conditions are met, MCAS software will initiate ***AND*** commands.

Most people don't understand that the FCC (and its internal MCAS software) is connected to only one AOA sensor. Like flipping a coin, that comes up heads twice, both crashes occurred because of a Captain's left AOA sensor. A Flight Officer's right AOA sensor that detected a stall would have activated MCAS as well, if FCC #2 was selected to be active for that flight.

Poor design of the original MCAS software used only one AOA sensor to activate it. Having 2 AOA sensors available on the 737 MAX, on a safety of flight mission critical system, amounts to criminal negligence in my opinion.

Who should be prosecuted among Boeing management for negligent homicide?
- Dennis Muilenburg, CEO and Chairman of the Board
- Keith Leverkuhn, General Manager of the 737 MAX program
- Michael Teal, Program Manager for the 737 MAX[41]

(These 3 individuals enforced that the design of the 737 MAX would not trigger flight simulator training time.)

Another person who worked at Boeing should also be prosecuted for murder as well:
- Mark Forkner

(This individual submitted a request to the F.A.A. to remove MCAS from written materials about the 737 MAX.)

When MCAS engages, it uses the electric STAB TRIM system that moves the horizontal stabilizer (large surface) using an electric motor to turn the jackscrew in the tail. Pilots only control the elevators (small surface) on the horizontal stabilizer by using the yoke and hydraulic actuators.

If pilots use the Pitch Trim thumb switches on top of the yoke, they can also command the horizontal stabilizer to move, by controlling the same electric motor MCAS uses, turning the jackscrew. Manual commands are not instantaneous, it takes time for the FCC to act upon the switch inputs before it sends a drive signal to the electric motor.

MCAS will engage for 10 seconds, wait 5 seconds while it waits for a response, before commanding another pitch down. (To be more

---

[41] The Seattle Times, "The inside story of MCAS: How Boeing's 737 MAX system gained power and lost safeguards", Dominic Gates and Mike Baker

specific, MCAS drives the horizontal stabilizer at 0.27° per second, for 9.26 seconds, for a total of 2.5002° movement.) Looking at the Pitch Trim Wheel, it is moving pretty fast when MCAS is in control.

It continues to ratchet a pitch down command after every waiting period of 5 seconds, until MCAS no longer senses a stall of the aircraft.

Final design parameters for MCAS software were to have it start with a strong command (2.5 units) pitch down, followed by 0.5 units pitch down commands after each 15 second interval.

Another huge design flaw of MCAS software was if the pilots used their Pitch Trim thumb switches on the yoke to try and move the horizontal stabilizer, that would reset the MCAS software.

If a pilot did NOT hold the thumb switches long enough to command 2.5 units of pitch up command to the horizontal stabilizer to counter the initial MCAS command, he/she would be in a losing battle of tug-of-war.

Only holding the thumb switches for a short time would reset MCAS, and MCAS would command 2.5 units of pitch down the next time it could.

A strange function of MCAS, it requires more force to pull the yoke back (nose up) and less force to push the yoke forward (nose down). When activated, MCAS software allows either pilot to apply a force of approximately 10 lbs. to move the yoke forward, pitch down position. Yet, when pulling the yoke back to the pitch up position, it can take 50 lbs. of force or more, to move the yoke. In the 737 MAX this increased resistance is applied by the Elevator Feel Computer – needed once Boeing did not have cables from the yoke attached to the elevators.

(The yoke only commands the elevators, through hydraulic actuators, to move a small surface on the trailing edge on each side of the horizontal stabilizer.)

There is only one way to disable MCAS commands, and that is to remove power from the STAB TRIM system, by turning the power switches on the pedestal to CUT OUT (OFF). The next step is to use the Pitch Trim Wheel located by the pilot's knees. Standard practice is to have the First Officer to turn the Pitch Trim Wheel, using a handle that will flip out, and then the wheel is cranked by hand. Many turns of the Pitch Trim Wheel results only in a small movement, plus, it is hard to turn. At high speeds, the Pitch Trim Wheel is physically impossible to turn.

Boeing had to update the software in 737 MAX and 737 NG simulators to accurately represent the force needed to manually turn the Pitch Trim Wheel. (Boeing had to patch the software twice, to get it right – inspires my confidence on how well they will patch the MCAS software correctly in one try.) Now that the Pitch Trim Wheel has the same forces applied to it as in real life, another problem was found. The F.A.A. is now studying the difficulty of turning that wheel, which leads to another question: "Do pilots possess the correct amount of upper body strength to move that wheel?"[42] (think female pilots and foreigner pilots who have a slender body frame)

Cables attached to the Pitch Trim Wheel, go through a series of pulleys, and run to the horizontal stabilizer, and move the jackscrew. At high speeds, the airflow over the horizontal stabilizer creates such a monumental force, that humans cannot physically move it.

Per Boeing design, they removed the "Yoke Jerk" function, it is no longer available on the 737 MAX 8. Anytime in the past, for all previously built 737's, pulling on the yoke hard, would disable electric STAB TRIM. While the 737 MAX 8 was being designed, someone at Boeing made a decision to disable the "Yoke Jerk" function.

---

[42] Wall Street Journal, "Boeing's Latest 737 Concern: Pilot's Physical Strength", Andy Pasztor and Andrew Tangel, 6/19/2019

The F.A.A. also allowed Boeing to disregard the Pitch Trim Limit Switches on the yoke from influencing the MCAS software – their sole purpose in life was to inhibit electric STAB TRIM commands when either pilot pulled the yoke all the way back. Almost every commercial aircraft has a yoke Pitch Trim Limit Switch linked to the yoke, to disable or remove STAB TRIM. Without a reference to MCAS in the differences training or in the Aircraft Flight Manual, that should also be considered a criminal act of negligence, resulting in hundreds of deaths. Because both flight crews relied on their previous training, information and experience, only to find out nothing they knew worked to disable the STAB TRIM from being used to override them by MCAS software.

Besides choosing any single AOA sensor to trigger MCAS, when Boeing converted to a glass cockpit in the 737 MAX 8, they also removed the dial indicators for the AOA that used to be on both sides of the instrument panel. Any operator can have them displayed on the glass panel, but purchasing this option can have an unintended consequence, mandatory full flight simulator training could be triggered. (Pilots would need training on what to do when they disagree.)

Another safety OPTION is to have a stand-alone indicator light on the instrument panel that illuminates when the two AOA sensors differ by more than 5.5°. The cost for this option is $30,000 per aircraft. However, if an airline chooses this option, it also can trigger mandatory full flight simulator training time as well (how is a pilot to react when this colored light illuminates). Plus, such a warning light is not linked to the MCAS software in any way.

<u>A general consensus among the Boeing engineers must have been that the AOA sensors were highly reliable</u>. People writing the software were separated from the people who maintain aircraft and had real world experience with AOA sensors. (My experience changing AOA sensors, or watching others change them, tells me they are not to be relied upon as a single source of failure for a critical safety system for an aircraft.)

Many U.S. commercial aircraft rely upon Rosemount Aerospace to manufacture AOA sensors. No one bothered to research this topic, because if they did, they would find out this sensor is a wink link no matter who manufactures it.

Occasionally AOA sensors look good on the outside but are wildly inaccurate inside, other times they are bent, and in a worst-case scenario – they just break off. Maybe it is because of their construction materials, physical design, or just because it is external to the airframe (although other probes are external to airframe, and rarely sustain damage.) Using this knowledge of unreliable AOA sensors, I would have used a second source of information to trigger MCAS software.

Someone at the F.A.A. made a determination that MCAS was not a "Highest Level of Risk System", thereby allowing only one AOA sensor to be used. Not only is it hard to fathom why MCAS software was not classified as "Highest Risk" it's hard to imagine why when Boeing had two sensors available, they only chose to use one!

One very important element of how MCAS software works has to do with the Elevator Feel Computer (EFC). One pilot, on the previous flight before JT610, was logged on the Cockpit Voice Recorder that he could not pull back on the yoke because it felt so heavy, i.e. it took more force to pull it back than he was able to exert by himself. MCAS sends a signal to the EFC to increase the force needed to move the yoke aft (nose up).

A confusion point has been introduced by Boeing in public statements trying to convince the general public that MCAS software is not new. Boeing management has said that MCAS software can also activate the spoiler to assist the pilots when they use the ailerons to roll the aircraft. Not True. The Flight Control Computer, where the MCAS software runs, actually has performed that function well before MCAS was invented.

Another way the CEO of Boeing has tried to "hide the ball" is to convince the general public that MCAS is nothing special, it is just part of the Speed Trim System. Nothing could be farther from the truth.

Speed Trim increases stability at low speeds. If the aircraft is at a low speed, it will point the nose slightly down using the horizontal stabilizer. MCAS software is significantly different, as it's used to correct for an unstable aircraft at higher speeds.

If a commercial airplane cannot land on a runway and is forced into a Go-Around, and keeps their speed low, Speed Trim can activate (if autopilot is NOT engaged). All commercial airliners slow down to land.

Again, the Speed Trim functions have long existed before the creation of MCAS software.

10. MCAS SOFTWARE – FLIGHT CRITICAL

Flight control software, like MCAS, by definition is "safety critical software".

Let me restate that Boeing has removed 2 avionics boxes, Stall Management / Yaw Damper (SMYD) Computers; they are not installed in the 737 MAX. Both SMYD computers have been a fixture in previous 737's, they were a stall warning system to both pilots in the cockpit. Removing these purely alerting systems and replacing them with a single AUTOMATED control system was brash. I have to remark here that Boeing put all of the software functions of the SMYD Computers into the already crowded FCC.

Boeing added specific hardware to the already existing 2 Flight Control Computers (FCC's). Then they supplied Collins Aerospace (the manufacturer of the FCC) with written software requirements so they could create and insert MCAS software into the FCC's, so it could control the pitch axis when an approaching stall is sensed.

So, to reiterate, Boeing took an existing FCC design, loaded it with the SMYD Computer software and then added to it MCAS software. (I suspect inside the FCC is an Intel 80286 CPU trying to perform all that extra work, and I equate that to a mule with luggage stacked 8 ft. high on its back, trekking along a trail that's too close to the side of a cliff.)

Instead of just a pure alerting system, as was provided by both SMYD Computers, now the FCC is a fully automated pitch control system when the 737 MAX detects the likelihood of a stall.

The F.A.A. has published Advisory Circular 20-115D titled "Airborne Software Development Assurance" on July 21, 2017. It recognizes RTCA DO-178C "Software Considerations in Airborne Systems and Equipment Certification" as one way to certify software in flight critical systems. (The F.A.A. published AC 20-115C, on July 19, 2013, and it says the same thing about RTCA DO-178C.)

There are other methods to certify software in critical flight safety systems, such as the one SAE publishes: ARP4754A "Guidelines for Development of Civil Aircraft and Systems".

All flight critical safety software will adhere to standards that have been published, no company just "wings" software development in aviation safety critical systems.

Both DO-178C and ARP4754A are complimentary, they both emphasize the same thing, just written differently.

The most important thing about this Chapter is to recognize that the above documents require a System Safety Analysis on the "**as-built**" system. In RTCA DO-178C, it declares that there are 5 categories of software, from Catastrophic to No Effect:

1. **Catastrophic**
Chances of this occurring are 1 in 1,000,000,000 flight hours
Extremely Improbable
Classified as Level "A"
(Multiple fatalities, <u>total destruction of aircraft</u>)

2. **Hazardous**
Chances of this occurring are 1 in 10,000,000 flight hours
Extremely Remote
Classified as Level "B"
(Small number of injuries and deaths)

3. **Major**
Chances of this occurring are 1 in 100,000 flight hours
Remote

4. **Minor**

5. **No Effect**

How can I emphasize that a System Safety Analysis (SSA) is required to be performed **AFTER** all the changes had been made to the MCAS software? Boeing performed an SSA before all of the changes were done to MCAS, merely revisited it a few times without doing a completely fresh analysis on if the MCAS software could cause an airplane crash. What possible software standard were they using to create MCAS that would allow that?

Many people confuse safety terms. I have experience as an OSHA Ground Safety Officer for a F.A.A. field office that included an aircraft hangar. Hopefully I can shed some light on how Boeing uses the word "critical" meaning one thing, but listeners hear something else.

There are two separate definitions of "critical" safety items in the aviation world. In software, which is covered in this chapter, "critical" relates to an objective, measurable quantity – an event that will occur once in 1,000,000,000 flight hours, i.e. catastrophic. (A movie buff may remember the "Princess Bride" were one villain repeats the word "inconceivable" many times for events that happen repeatedly. Boeing must have thought MCAS software driving a 737 MAX purposely into the Earth was not just extremely improbable but was "inconceivable".)

When it comes to <u>aircraft manufacturers</u>, <u>governmental regulatory bodies</u>, and <u>airline operators</u>, applying that term to an airplane as a whole: "critical" is subjective. Any of these 3 groups can determine what item is critical to them, and it won't apply to the other 2 groups. If any one of those three groups determine something is essential to flight safety, they classify it as "critical". Yet, one group may not take another's definition as essential, but they can classify that same item as non-essential.[43]

---

[43] The Star, "Why the 737 Max should never fly again", David Olive, 6/15/2019

Boeing is trying to play this semantic word game when they talk about MCAS software, and what they subjectively identify as essential safety of flight, i.e., "critical". Boeing's CEO, Dennis Muilenburg, has personally classified the lack of the AOA DISAGREE warning as not essential to safety of flight, so to him this lack of a safety warning is not a critical item.

Dennis Muilenburg at the annual shareholder meeting in Chicago went so far as to state that the AOA DISAGREE warning was secondary, supplemental information, not part of critical safety data.[44]

Our First Amendment to the U.S. Constitution allows citizens the right to free speech. So, Boeing's CEO can say anything he wants about MCAS when he is not under oath. In my opinion, the flying public should have a right to know what the meaning of the words "safe" and "critical", as pertaining to flying inside an aircraft.

QUESTION: HOW MANY 737 MAX FLIGHT HOURS WERE LOGGED BEFORE THE FIRST CRASH (JT610)?

In the U.S. a total of just over 50,000 flights (averaging 3 flight hours each) had been logged safely since delivery of the 737 MAX until they were grounded on March 13, 2019.[45]

QUESTION: SHOULD MCAS SOFTWARE BE CLASSIFIED AS CATASTROPHIC?

Boeing's internal System Safety Analysis, with no participation or monitoring from the F.A.A.,[46] determined that MCAS software fell into the category defined as just "Hazardous" – or Level "B" software.

---

[44] Wall Street Journal, "Boeing Signals Additional 737 MAX Airliner Software Problem", Andy Pastor and Andrew Tangel, 4/30/2019

[45] Wall Street Journal, "Between Two Deadly Crashes, Boeing Moved Haltingly to Make 737 MAX Fixes", Andy Pasztor, Andrew Tangel and Alison Sider, 4/1/2019

[46] The Hill, "FAA didn't review 737 MAX system assessment before crashes", John

Originally, MCAS had a maximum authority of 0.6 units of horizontal stabilizer movement. Add to that the probability of a commercial airliner needing to make a high-speed turn at full power times the chance that MCAS will fail at that exact time, and Boeing estimated this will occur once every 223 trillion flight hours.[47]

What Boeing did not do, was a failure to recalculate those odds after losing the only redundant sensor (vertical accelerometer), increasing MCAS authority to command 2.5 units of trim, and allowing it to do so many times. Never even comprehending the flight profile of 737 MAX take-off.

After trying to understand how Boeing employees arrived at their conclusion of classifying MCAS as Level "B" software, the best I can come up with is: *"Software inside the previous SMYD Computer was classified as Level "B" since it was only an alerting system, and since the FCC is replacing it, it should get the same category, right?"*

After the first crash, JT610, this evaluation of software classification should have been seriously revisited, it wasn't. Then the second crash occurred, ET302, over 50 countries grounded the 737 MAX fleet. Finally, the F.A.A. grounded the U.S. fleet 1 day after almost all of the other countries had already taken such action.

It took over 2 months, but Boeing has revisited the original System Safety Analysis in May 2019, and so has the F.A.A., and they both arrived at that original decision, that MCAS software is not in the *Catastrophic* software category.

Even though I did teach RTCA DO-178 to F.A.A. Airworthiness Safety Inspectors while I was at the F.A.A. Academy in Oklahoma City, facts I have retained in my memory are stale. Leanna Rierson has

---

[47] The Seattle Times, "The inside story of MCAS: How Boeing's 737 MAX system gained power and lost safeguards" Dominic Gates and Mike Baker, 6/22/2019

written an excellent book on RTCA DO-178C, titled "Developing Safety Critical Software"; I read her book to give me knowledge on the current state of writing aviation software.

To anyone wanting a more in-depth analysis than I provide, or to prove me wrong about software, this is a must-read book. (In October of 2019, she is supposed to be releasing another book on this topic.) After reading this book, I've been able to refresh myself on flight safety software.

If any technical geeks are reading this, they must be asking what programming language was probably used in the FCC's? In my opinion it is the Ada programming language. It was developed by the Department of Defense (D.O.D), as a standard software language across their broad scope of computer products. One source of mine told me that Ada is the first object-orientated programming language. Leanna Rierson mentioned it was named after Ada Lovelace, the first true computer programmer. (Airbus uses the SPARK programming language.)

All I know and have experience with is Assembly Language while I was a D.O.D employee; it is a very low-level programming language; it is CPU specific and is really fast.

Following any published standard for flight critical software, it must be traceable, so every task performed has documentation about it, for traceability. This includes; the overall planning document, design requirements, every problem report, validation testing (errors will show a software requirement was incomplete), and verification testing (errors stemming from writing the software code imperfectly).

Some government entity needs to analyze all of this documentation for MCAS software, because Boeing has failed in at least 2 instances I personally know of (actually it was their vendor, Collins Aerospace).

First, the MCAS Software had a requirement specifying that anytime the 2 sensors disagreed by 10°, an **AOA DISAGREE** warning would be displayed on the PFD's (which Collins Aerospace manufactures, they also do the entire glass cockpit in the 737 MAX). This warning is only displayed on airplanes that purchased the "Error Notification Kit" which was optional. In the Aircraft Flight Manual supplied to all 737 MAX airplane operators, there is a reference to this warning message, so it was supposed to be on all 737 MAX airplanes.

Second, a more insidious problem with MCAS software, has already been rectified.

To develop flight critical software, all failure probabilities and how they are handled need to be specified in the software requirements and verified after the hardware and software is completed.

Boeing let slip into the wild, in every 737 MAX airplane they built, MCAS software that did not handle a flap switch failure correctly. Flap switches are inside each wing, need to be physically moved around when installed or replaced, to be accurate, then tightened down. I've done this task as well. Looking at the real-time FDR values, the flap switch is positioned correctly for each flap handle setting in the cockpit, before being permanently installed.

Three things are required before MCAS software engages the FCC to move the horizontal stabilizer autonomously, besides the AOA sensor:
1. The Flap switches in the wings have to indicate flaps have been fully retracted
2. Weight-on-wheels switches have to indicate wheels are not on the ground, and switches activated by the landing gear doors shows they have been closed: in the cockpit that means seeing three green lights indicating "wheels up"
3. Airplane speed exceeds 180 knots (+/-)

Collins Aerospace corrected a problem with handling the occurrence of a flap switch failure with a Service Bulletin on January 25, 2019.[48] For those outside the aviation community, a Service Bulletin is Voluntary. Each airline will have their own Quality Assurance department, one of their duties is to evaluate every Service Bulletin and decide on which ones they will implement in their fleet and which ones to disregard. (Anything complicated can be referred to the airlines' engineering department for guidance.)

Even when Boeing did issue a Service Bulletin after the first crash of the 737 MAX, JT610, they issued the procedures for handling Runaway Trim – it was voluntary. Only when the next day went by, did the F.A.A. incorporate Boeing's Service Bulletin into an Airworthiness Directive, then Boeing's Service Bulletin became mandatory.

To not handle a flap switch failure in the originally written MCAS software is inexcusable.

Software must be operable in all foreseeable conditions, per published standards for flight safety critical software; it must handle fault detection and handling.

THINK ABOUT IT:

Did any airlines include this MCAS software patch into their fleet?

What other software errors are embedded in the MCAS software?

---

[48] The Washington Post, "Boeing's 737 Max design contains fingerprints of hundreds of suppliers", Douglas MacMillan and Aaron Gregg, 4/5/2019

11. HOW FLIGHT CONTROLS WORK

Most of my earlier writing took for granted the reader was familiar with aviation, and the moveable surfaces on the airplane. In this chapter I will briefly explain movable flight control surfaces on commercial airplanes and what they do. Anyone who is a professional pilot can skip this section.

Everyone should be familiar with the yoke in the cockpit, its position is forward of both pilots, and is sort of between their legs.

Ailerons are part of the wing surface, located on the trailing edge of each wing, near its center.

Turning the yoke to the right or left moves the ailerons, which in turn make the aircraft either roll to the left or to the right in flight. One aileron will move up while the opposite one moves down in sync with one another.

By the feet of each pilot there are pedals (rudder pedals) that will move the rudder left or right, which is on the trailing edge of the vertical stabilizer (that is the part of the tail that sticks straight up, about 30 feet into the sky, it looks like the aircraft's tail fin). Also, on the rudder are trim tabs, used by both the autopilot and a yaw damper computer (or FCC), to make small adjustments, so the tail of the aircraft stays aligned with the nose of the aircraft and does not fishtail. Yaw damper commands are now done by the FCC in the 737 MAX.

Moving the horizontal stabilizer can be accomplished by turning the jackscrew in the tail, by physical movement of attached cables, or sending drive signals to its electric motor. It is comprised of two large surfaces that resembles a mini wing, located on each side of the tail fin.

Elevators are located on each side of the horizontal stabilizer, on the trailing edge. Pilots move this small surface by moving the yoke either forwards or backwards.

Flaps in large commercial aircraft operate differently than in smaller aircraft. Small aircraft take-off and land at much slower speeds, so they do not need as much lift as a large aircraft. Normally flaps are a single surface, one on each wing, near the fuselage, on the trailing edge of the wing. Flaps are extended for landing and take-off, they increase lift. Once airborne, the flaps are retracted, until it is time for landing.

Large commercial aircraft have flaps on both the trailing edge AND leading edge of the wings, between the fuselage and engines. In concert with the flaps are Slats, located on the leading edge of the wings, between the engines and wing tips. When the flaps are extended, so are the slats. Considering a fully loaded 737 MAX 8 weighs more than 180,000 lbs., it needs all the lift it can get for take-off.

One other thing large commercial aircraft have that small private aircraft don't is spoilers. Depending on aircraft size, there will usually be either 6 or 8 spoilers.

Spoilers have two uses; one is to dump airspeed by restricting airflow over the tops of the wing, the other time they can be used is during an aircraft roll (lateral changes in heading). Using the spoilers does affect the lift, reducing it when deployed, and doing so also increases the AOA that the aircraft will stall at.

Above are brief descriptions on how flight control surfaces work in commercial airplanes.

The following inform the reader on a few other concepts that may be helpful to understand flying as well.

Mach Trim is active when the 737 MAX 8 is flown between 0.61 Mach and 0.86 Mach (high speed). The FCC's move the elevators on the horizontal stabilizer to keep the airplane within its flight limits when being flown without autopilot (Mach Trim is software in the FCC).

When the airplane increases speed the Mach Trim software provides nose up commands, as the Mach number increases.[49]

Speed Trim is active at low speeds, above 100 knots till about 180 knots in the 737 MAX. Residing inside the FCC's is software that acts like an augmentation system to keep the aircraft stable at low speeds by moving the horizontal stabilizer. (All commercial airplanes slow down when landing.) There is a table for Speed Trim commands, specifying "x" number of units of trim, for moving Pitch Trim down at a corresponding airspeed. These commands are applied incrementally; it only functions when the autopilot is not engaged. A failsafe for the Speed Trim system is the Pitch Limit Cutout Switches, so if the yoke is moved to its extreme position, the Speed Trim system deactivates.

A coordinated turn is when the pilot uses the yoke's two functions, plus the rudder pedals, all at once.

Turning the aircraft using the yoke (left or right) moves the ailerons putting the aircraft in a roll, which also puts the aircraft into a dive. At the same time, the pilots also pull back on the yoke moving the elevators to increase the lift, so the aircraft does not lose altitude during the turn. The tail of the aircraft has the tendency to swing out during a turn, i.e., fishtail, so the rudder is used in a turn (left or right) to keep the tail of the aircraft aligned with the nose – hence a coordinated turn.

Any lateral motion left or right, without using the elevators will cause loss of altitude, by itself.

Back when the 737-200 was being manufactured, they included in that airplane's AFM a procedure called the "roller-coaster maneuver".[50] [51]

---

[49] Satcom guru (website), "Stabilizer Trim", Peter Lemme, 11/12/2018

[50] Business Insider, "A little-known quirk on the Boeing 737 may have made things difficult for the pilots of the crashed Ethiopian Airlines flight", Benjamin Zhang, 4/6/2019

[51] The Seattle Times, "Why Boeing's emergency directions may have failed to save 737 MAX", Dominic Gates, 4/3/2019

There are conditions where a 737 may have tremendous pressure on the horizontal stabilizer, preventing the flight crews from manually trimming it with the Pitch Trim Wheels in the cockpit. To allow movement, one pilot pitches the aircraft down with the yoke, alleviating the air pressure, so the other pilot can crank the Pitch Trim Wheel a little bit. Repeating this procedure repeatedly will eventually get the horizontal stabilizer back into a correct position, hence the name "roller-coaster" – the airplane pitches up and down, over and over, while one pilot is moving the Pitch Trim Wheel whenever the airplane is nose down.

Both aircraft that crashed, JT610 and ET302, did not have enough altitude to perform this roller-coaster maneuver.

Trimming the aircraft is actually integral to MCAS software, so it is important to understand.

If both autopilots were to become inoperative during a flight and the pilots had to hand fly the aircraft to the destination for hours, they would eventually become physically worn out, due to fighting the yoke to keep the aircraft straight and level. Winds aloft are strong, and if not adjusted for, will turn the aircraft off-course.

Separate trim controls move both the rudder and the horizontal stabilizer.

Rudder Trim is controlled by a wheel in the center console, between the pilots, and because it does not affect MCAS, so that is all I will say about it.

Pitch Trim is another animal, MCAS software can control it, along with the pilots and the autopilot system.

Pitch Trim is used in flight to counter-balance winds aloft, so the flight profile of the aircraft can fly level, without having to move the yoke from its null position.

There are five ways to control Pitch Trim. Four of those ways use the electric motor that drives the jackscrew which moves the horizontal stabilizer; the other one uses a more direct way – cables attached to the jackscrew.

Earlier I described Speed Trim, which is a software function inside the FCC's that drives the movement of the horizontal stabilizer, using the electric motor attached to the jackscrew, at only lower speeds.

Another method is when the autopilot is engaged, it basically sends drive signals to the electric motor attached to the jackscrew, which will move the horizontal stabilizer up and down. MCAS software should not work when the autopilot is engaged. (I suspect MCAS kicks off the autopilot before it activates, and then prevents it from being selected again until the airplane is "in trim" condition.)

Using the Pitch Trim thumb wheel switches on top of the yoke, the horizontal stabilizer can be moved. How much movement is dictated by how long a time the thumb wheel switches are pushed, either forward or back (and there is a slight delay between moving the thumb switches and the time the horizontal stabilizer moves in the 737 MAX).

When the electric motor no longer works, or if the pilots kill power to STAB TRIM by turning its two switches to CUT OUT (OFF) on the pedestal in the cockpit, then there is a Pitch Trim Wheel, located by the pilot's knees, that is used to turn the horizontal stabilizer manually. Cables are used to do this. It is evident in the cockpit that cables are attached to the Pitch Trim Wheel, because every time the horizontal stabilizer moves, the Pitch Trim Wheel turns.

Lastly on STAB TRIM, added to the 737 MAX 8, <u>without pilot knowledge</u>, it is controlled by MCAS software. When all the pre-conditions are met, it activates. Sensing a stall, it points the nose in a pitch down attitude using the horizontal stabilizer to increase speed, and thereby generating more lift.

One by product of more speed is the Pitch Trim Wheel gets harder to turn, because the forces of air rushing over the horizontal stabilizer become greater. At some point the speed of the aircraft makes turning the Pitch Trim Wheel impossible.

Focusing our attention to the elevators, they are indirectly controlled by the yoke on the 737 MAX 8.

Pulling back on the yoke sends a signal to the hydraulic actuators, that actually moves the small surfaces located on the trailing edge of the stabilizer, called the "elevators", and they them move up and down.

An Elevator Feel Computer was developed because somewhere in time the cables from the yoke were replaced with signals, and the pilots needed some sort of feedback when they pushed or pulled on the yoke.

In normal operation, about 10 lbs. of force are needed to push the yoke forward, and to pull it back.

However, when MCAS is activated, the pilots are in for a rude shock. Pushing the yoke forward still requires about 10 lbs. of force, pulling the yoke back to pull up, requires about 50 lbs. of force or more. MCAS utilizes the Elevator Feel Computer to increase the force needed to pull back on the yoke. Hopefully, both pilots are physically fit, been working out in the gym with weights, and have been running to build up their endurance.

If anyone has given CPR in the real world, they understand the idea I'm trying to convey. Even with adrenalin pumping through your veins, the person who is giving chest compressions on the lifeless body starts to tire quickly from performing CPR on a person for more than just a few minutes.

Noted in the Ethiopian Air ET302 crash is a phenomenon called "elevator blowback". Once the elevator is at a steep angle at high speed, the wind over the elevators actually overcomes the hydraulic actuators used to move them. The air movement creates such force that the elevators are blown back to a neutral position, even though the pilots have the yoke pulled all the way back, hence the term "elevator blowback".

12. WHAT IS LONGITUDINAL INSTABILITY?

Trying to compete with Airbus for a more fuel-efficient aircraft, Boeing took a third generation 737, and modified it to be a fourth generation 737. Doing so was difficult, as the new engines were larger, and each jet engine weighed 600 lbs. more than the one used on the 737 NG-800 (literally double the weight and thrust of the engines used on the original 737-100).

Airbus decided on using a CFM LEAP 1A jet engine. Boeing had to settle for a CFM LEAP 1B jet engine; it was smaller and less fuel efficient but could be attached to a 737 wing and still maintain sufficient ground clearance.

Even though the 3rd generation 737 NG airframe was not radically changed like what Boeing did to the 737 MAX, the placement of the engines in front the wings did alter its aerodynamics slightly.

The 737 MAX became unstable longitudinally (it would pitch up in normal flight) because of the placement of the engine nacelles.

Placing the engines so far forward on the 737 MAX altered the airplanes Center of Gravity (CG), moving it too close to its Center of Lift – creating a slightly unstable airplane in flight.

Let me explain… an airplane has 3 axis of movement: Pitch (longitude), Roll (lateral), and Yaw (heading). A mathematician may look at it like an X-Y-Z problem.

Yaw is easy to understand: an aircraft will fishtail in the sky without correction in the Yaw axis. Aircraft engineers concentrate on controlling the tail of the airplane, so passengers don't become nauseous and throw-up. Anyone outside of aviation would call the "Yaw axis" the "Heading axis", because passengers concentrate on where the nose of the aircraft is pointing.

On the 737 MAX the Roll and Yaw are aerodynamically stable. Not so with Pitch.

> **QUESTION: WHY DID BOEING ALLOW THIS 4ᵀᴴ GENERATION 737 MAX AIRPLANE TO HAVE UNSTEADY PITCH?**

In my opinion, it was fuel economy that was the driving force behind the logic in manufacturing an unstable airplane by Boeing.

To make an airplane steady in its Pitch axis, a small force is applied to the horizontal stabilizer to keep it flying level. Putting such a small pressure on the tail of the aircraft creates drag, reducing fuel economy.

Looking at the specifications of the A320NEO's jet engines (LEAP 1A) that Airbus uses, a reader may notice that the bypass ration is 11:1. Whereas the 737 MAX has the LEAP 1B with a bypass ration of 9:1. The larger the bypass ratio, all things being equal, the more fuel efficient it is.

Boeing had to increase the fuel efficiency of the 737 MAX's airframe to be compete with the Airbus A320NEO. Hence, they manufacture the 737 MAX with an unstable Pitch axis – so there is no pressure applied to the horizontal stabilizer, no drag, increasing fuel economy.

In doing so, Boeing had to control the Pitch axis; it's accomplished by MCAS software inside the Flight Control Computer.

All airplanes will pitch up when the throttles are advanced, in the 737 MAX it is even more pronounced.

13. REDESIGN OF 737 INTO 737 MAX 8

Although some of this material was covered piecemeal in the preceding chapters, a more comprehensive view is presented here.

Originally designed in the early 1960's, the 737 was based on the 707 and 727 aircraft. Its first flight occurred in April 1967, back when most Americans had only Black & White television sets and electronics used tubes not transistors. A little over half of the 727 airframes structure was retained in the 737 to shorten design time (approximately 65% of those previous airframes were used on the first 737). Considering more than 50% of the original 737 was based on the 707 and 727, it is closer to a sixty-year-old design.

Americans flying in a 737 MAX 8 are basically flying in an aircraft designed more than 50 years ago, with tweaks made every few years. Would you climb into a "new" 1975 Ford 150 pickup with a stranger driving, knowing the seats were new, as was the dashboard and motor, but the underlying frame was essentially as old as your grandmother? Keeping in mind all the improvements in crash safety made over the 4 plus decades since that Ford pickup was built? Remember, it basically looks exactly the same as a 1975 Ford pickup. It's still a new pickup, but, using 45-year-old blueprints from the Smithsonian Museum to build it.

Way back in 1975 the sticker price on a Ford 150 pickup truck was $4,500. Today, Ford can produce that exact same truck for less than $4,000. Seatbelts weren't mandatory, side windows needed a mechanical crank handle, it did not have hardly any safety features, and its fuel mileage was pitiful considered to today's vehicles. Can anyone remember how many U.S. highway fatalities there were in 1975? The U.S. had 45,500 people die in highway accidents that year.

A no frills Ford 150 pickup costs $28,000 in 2019. With a U.S. population increase of over 50% in the years between 1975 and 2019, there are fewer individuals dying on the road today because of car safety regulations being enforced.

Do we as a society really want airplane manufacturers in a race to the bottom, so we can have the lowest ticket prices? I think not. When I get on an aircraft, I don't want[52] to consider whether I'll trade my safety for a lower ticket price. All aircraft that fly should be safe, but today is a new era, and Boeing is paving a new frontier for all others to follow, focus on profits and hope it's safe enough. Boeing's Public Relations probably have a script they pull out when one of their airplanes crash:
1. Blame the pilots
2. Deny everything
3. Admit nothing
4. Lie
5. If all else fails, make counter accusations to muddy the waters. (Similar to what Boeing did in 1991 after the first crash of a 737, and again when another 737 crashed in 1994 for the same reason.)

Boeing engineers designed the original 737 to be a short-haul commercial jetliner used to only haul passengers. Going back in time, remember that airports in the U.S. did not have the modern Jetways used to board modern aircraft today. Instead this aircraft was designed to be low to the ground, having folding stairs incorporated into the main door, to load and unload passengers onto the tarmac.

In March 2018, Boeing announced the 10,000th 737 aircraft rolled out of the factory floor.

It may be hard to believe, but there was a 737-100, 737-200, 737-300, 737-400, 737-500; they then introduced Next Generation aircraft: 737-600, 737-700, 737-800, 737-900. Finally, and most recently, they

---

[52] New York Times, "The Boeing 737 Max Crisis Is a Leadership Failure", Jim Hall and Peter Goelz, 7/17/2019

started selling the 737 MAX 8; its maiden flight was on January 29, 2016. (Boeing is still developing the 737 MAX 10.)

The 737-100 engines were not placed near the tail as in the 727 because they wanted to lighten the fuselage, so it could accommodate 3 passenger seats on each side of the aisle.

Engineers originally placed the Nacelles (pods holding the engine) underneath the wings and low to the ground. Two advantage to this were shorter landing gear, making it easier for loading / unloading passengers, while also making ground inspections of engines by maintenance easier. Baggage handlers could just toss bags into the aircraft without a ladder.

Nacelles have changed over the years, with the 737 MAX 8 being quite a departure over previous designs (affecting aerodynamics). Even the wings were changed slightly, with split -tip winglets, to achieve better aerodynamics.

In the 737 MAX, the nacelles (housing the LEAP 1B engines made by CFM) were too big to be mounted normally. Design teams eventually agreed to place the nacelles more forward and higher on the wing to improve ground clearance, so much so that the top of the engine appears to be peeking above the wing. Placing the engines forward and higher had an unintended consequence, this made the engine thrust interact with the airflow under the wing.

Needing 2 per airplane, a pair of these engines cost $30 million (U.S.) about a 3rd of the aircraft cost.

	LEAP-1A A320NEO Airbus	LEAP-1B 737 MAX Boeing	LEAP-1C C919 Comac
Engine Thrust	24,500 to 35,000	23,000 to 28,000	27,900 to 30,000
Engine Weigth - lbs.	6,592 (wet)	6,130 (dry)	8,675 (wet)
Engine Intake Fan Size	78"	69"	77"
Bypass Ratio	11:1	9:1	11:1
Engine Length	131"	124"	177"

Changes to the aircraft's aerodynamics, along with non-standard engine placement had another consequence. At full power and with flaps up, the conditions of take-off, the aircraft could stall. (Stall occurs when not enough air is moving on top of the wing correctly, so it loses lift, and stalls in midair, i.e. no longer moving up – dropping like a stone.)

Besides fuel efficient engines, Boeing also changed the wing design, and replaced all of the mechanical instruments with a glass cockpit.

Comparison between the original 737 design and the 737 MAX 8

	737-100	difference	737 MAX 8
Length	94' 0"	35' 8"	129' 8"
Wing Span	93' 0"	24" 10"	117' 10"
Wheel Base	41' 5"	9' 9"	51' 2"
Fuel Capacity - gallons	6,878	same	6,878
Seating	149	40	189
Empty Weight	113,999	31,401	145,400
Maximum Take-off Weight - lbs.	153,499	27,730	181,229
Cruise Speed	0.785 Mach	same	0.785 Mach
Range	1,720 nm	1,830	3,550 nm
Engines	JT8D-7		LEAP-1B
Engine Thrust	14,000 lbs.	14,000	28,000 lbs.
Engine Weight	3,205 (dry)	2,925	6,130 (dry)
Engine Intake	40"	29	69"

Looking at the comparison table, it's easy to see that these are two different aircraft, not a simple variation from the original design. To me, it is unconscionable how the F.A.A. granted a Derivative Type

Certificate to the 737 MAX 8. It may be a derivative of a derivative (the 737 NG 800), but not a derivative of the original 737 Type Certificate. It is not legal to issue a Derivative Type Certificate based on a Derivative Type Certificate.

I have been taught in a course conducted at the F.A.A. Academy, located at the Mike Monroney Aeronautical Center, how to interpret federal regulations. May I reference the reader to 14 CFR 21.19 "Changes requiring a new Type Certificate" – if there is an extensive change to the original Type Certificate of either Design, Power, Thrust, or Weight, then the new design requires a new Type Certificate.

Compared to the original 737-100, the 737 MAX is 35 ft longer, a wingspan increase of 24 ft, increased empty weight of 31,000 lbs., and doubles the original thrust from the engines of 14,000 lbs. Any rational reader must agree that those specification differences are extensive and therefore requires a new Type Certificate. (If Boeing did what was required by federal regulation, then all 737 MAX pilots would require a new rating on their pilot's license and require full flight simulator training on that airplane. Pilots on previous 737 could not fly the 737 MAX without a new type rating on their pilot's license.)

Comparing just the engines is impressive, the 737 MAX 8 engines are twice the size, weight, and thrust of the original engines. Because of the fuel-efficient engines and airframe redesign, the 737 MAX 8 can fly more than double the distance of the original 737-100.

The air inlet of the LEAP 1B is huge, to accommodate added air that bypasses the "hot section" of the engine to boost performance. A second advantage of having such a large intake fan portion of the engine is that it helps in noise reduction.

Considering the Airbus A320NEO is 5% more fuel efficient by design because the Airbus airplane has an almost 10" larger intake fan than a 737 MAX. Boeing had to make up that difference somewhere, and it was by designing an unstable aircraft in the pitch axis.

In my opinion, the greatest challenges Boeing managers had while they were designing and building the 737 MAX was how to hold costs down by firing and laying off experienced employees and replacing them with cheap contractors; meet self-imposed scheduled deadlines; and avoid pilots needing a new type rating to fly it.

Boeing has put pressure on their engineering staff, to churn out the 737 MAX, and not repeat the debacle of the 787, which had costs overruns of billions and delivered 3 years late.

One example exemplifies this horrible situation: when a Boeing AR required testing of the fire-suppression system on the new CFM LEAP 1B jet engines on the 737 MAX.[53] He presented his testing method to his manager and was told to do it cheaper and quicker. Instead he convened a meeting of his certification unit employees (engineers) at Boeing and explained his methodology to them. Looking to see if someone could find a better way to test the fire-suppression system than his idea: all of them agreed with his approach.

Going back to management, he explained again that there were no shortcuts, and that everyone in his unit agreed. Management disagreed. Then management brought in a certification engineer who did not work at Boeing to review the testing procedure that was proposed; the outside expert agreed with Boeing's AR. Only after hearing from someone outside Boeing, did management greenlight the original testing procedure.

A delay ensued, where the AR who required proper testing of the fire-suppression system was transferred to another unit, general engineering. He was not given a job description or any work – an example to the other AR's to play ball, or worse would happen to them.

---

[53] Esquire, "Maybe We Shouldn't Leave It to Boeing to say Whether Boeing Planes Are Safe", Charles P. Pierce, 5/6/2019

Please dwell on this, Boeing did not want to do a live-fire testing of the fire-suppression system for **NEW** engines. It's incomprehensible how Boeing is telling the public that safety comes first, after reading a story like this.

Cost cutting at Boeing did not just focus on keeping certification time and expenses down, but there were wholesale layoffs in departments needed for airplane safety. "Flight Crew Operations" was one such department, this is the group that managed how 737 MAX pilots interacted with software and cockpit controls. Staffing was 30 certification engineers at first, but, was cut to 15 by Boeing bean-counters.[54]

These were the people who could have insisted that there would have to be a displayed message on the pilot's glass cockpit whenever MCAS was active. (Similar to the A/P message displayed when the autopilot is engaged, it could have just been the letters MCAS in green displayed on the top of the PFD when MCAS was actively moving the horizontal stabilizer.)

Focusing on cost reduction Boeing let go engineers making $150,000 – $200,000 per year; these engineers made up the backbone of their engineering departments. Replacements came in as contractors, from HCL Technologies Limited – based in India, for $9 an hour.[55] Basically, it works out to 10% of what Boeing was paying their talented and experienced engineers in the States. (Boeing pays $35 - $40 an hour to contract engineers who live inside the U.S.)

A very old proverb states "you get what you pay for".

---

[54] Bloomberg, "Former Boeing Engineers Say Relentless Cost-Cutting Sacrificed Safety", Peter Robison, 5/9/2019

[55] Bloomberg, "Boeing's 737 Max Software Outsourced to $9-an-hour Engineers", Peter Robison, 6/28/2019

Politics extend to business deals, as I personally know. After paying a lobbyist to sit down and chat over lunch with the F.A.A. Administrator (a long time ago) about F.A.A. lay-offs, as a union official I was presented with a Hobson's Choice. Get what I wanted if I dropped my objections to a $120 million aircraft purchase wanted by F.A.A. officials (they wanted half a dozen Lear jets and a few Challenger airplanes for their government fleet), of course I let the government spend tax dollars to keep approximately 120 jobs safe. My cost analysis may have been wrong, paying $1 million per job, but I'd have to look 60 employees in the eye and let them know I failed and that we all lost our jobs.

India purchased 100 of the 737 MAX 8 aircraft, after Boeing agreed to outsource many of their engineers, quid-pro-quo, I hire your employees and you buy my aircraft. Boeing agreed to invest $1.7 billion into India's ventures, and subsequently won a very large order from India.

Those cheap contractors in India have no idea about aerospace, or a culture rooted deeply in aviation safety.

Boeing is not alone in hiring cheap contractors, Collins Aerospace had 400 contractors working in India for them in 2010, exactly the same time they were building and writing code for the FCC to be used inside the 737 MAX.

One of the things that HCL Technologies Limited specializes in is object-oriented programming. The software used inside most of Collins Aerospace products probably uses the Ada programming language (since they sell so many of their products to our military), which is the first object-oriented programming language, predating C++ and Java.

14. FULL FLIGHT SIMULATOR TRAINING SHOULD BE REQUIRED

When the F.A.A. creates a Flight Standardization Board (FSB), it has the purpose of determining training on a new aircraft including a supposedly derivative aircraft, like the 737 MAX. Because the FSB determined the 737 MAX airplane was similar enough to the 737 NG-800, it was decided that Level "B" training would be all that is required. (Level "B" training can be accomplished on a computer, laptop, or iPad.)

The FSB that certified the 737 MAX was good to go with only iPad training was led by Stacy Klein[56], who had a background as a commercial pilot for only 6 years. William Schubbe was also on that FSB team.[57]

I know of only three 737 MAX full motion flight simulators (level "D") in the world. One is owned by Boeing – located in Miami[58], not Renton WA.; one is in Canada; the other was purchased by Ethiopian Air. Boeing only has a stationary simulator near its manufacturing location in Renton, WA. (American Airlines, as well as Southwest Airlines have orders placed for 737 MAX full motion flight simulators to be delivered to them by the end of 2019.)

One major difference between the 737 MAX and 737 NG (NG = Next Generation) aircraft simulators, beside MCAS software, is the cockpit glass panels. The 737 NG simulator has 5 normal size individual LCD screens, while the 737 MAX has 4 very large LCD

---

[56] Bloomberg, "Former Boeing Engineers Say Relentless Cost-Cutting Sacrificed Safety", Peter Robison, 5/9/2019

[57] New York Times, "Boeing Built Deadly Assumptions Into 737 MAX, Blind to a Late Design Change", Jack Nicas, Natalie Kitroeff, David Gelles, and James Glanz, 6/1/2019

[58] Wall Street Journal, "Inside the Effort to Fix the Troubled Boeing 737 MAX", Scott McCartney, 6/5/2019

screens. Information displayed on the 737 MAX 8 simulator is not in the same places as items displayed on the 737 NG simulator.

Boeing had previously said no full motion flight simulator training was needed for pilots flying the 737 MAX, pilots could climb into a 737 NG simulator and thereby get trained on the 737 MAX every year.

Pilots trying to recreate what happened on Ethiopian Air ET302 in a 737 NG full motion flight simulator were not successful in preventing a simulated third crash.[59][60]

A Boeing spokesman on 5/17/2019 announced that Boeing had just made available to manufacturers of 737 MAX flight simulators the needed corrections so they can duplicate conditions produced by MCAS software.[61]

QUESTION: DOES THE 737 NG FLIGHT SIMULATOR DISPLAY THE "AOA DISAGREE" WARNING?

Simulator training time is expensive, and every pilot who flies the 737 MAX 8 should be required to have it. Southwest Airlines put a value of $1 million dollars per airframe[62], if they were forced to give each of their pilots the mandatory full flight simulator training, over the lifetime of the aircraft.

Purchasing a separate full motion flight simulator costs approximately $10 million dollars over the life of the airplane besides the upfront purchase price of $15 million[63]. Simulator training staff and

---

[59] The Seattle Times, "Why Boeing's emergency directions may have failed to save 737 MAX", Dominic Gates, 4/3/2019

[60] The Seattle Times, "How much was pilot error a factor in the Boeing 737 MAX crashes", Dominic Gates, 5/15/2019

[61] New York Times, "Boeing discovers flaw in sought after 737 MAX simulator, the same kind that Ethiopian Airlines had", Natalie Kitroeff, 5/17/2019

[62] The Seattle Times, "The inside story of MCAS: How Boeing's 737 MAX system gained power and lost safeguards", Dominic Gates and Mike Baker, 6/22/2019

maintenance costs are not cheap. Adding the costs to purchase a flight simulator and maintain it comes to $25 million; then for each 737 MAX airplane in the fleet, increase that cost by $1 million for each airframe the airline purchased. Expensive.

To attend full flight simulator training, it typically takes 21 classroom hours of instruction, and at least one session on a full motion flight simulator for a minimum of 4 hours (each hour costs up to $1,000).[64] Recommendations are for 10 hours of simulator training for each pilot. Travel time, training time, and you must remember each airline incurs a cost penalty for having pilots miss a week of work for this training. Expensive.

Pilots are required to physically carry a license while they are flying, listing all of the aircraft they are "type rated" to fly. Any pilot with a 737 type rating can fly any version of the 737 aircraft. Requiring a separate type rating for the 737 MAX would require pilots to be trained on both the normal 737 and the 737 MAX; each pilot would have two type ratings on their license.

A separate issue from **mandatory** full flight simulator training, American Airlines announced in April 2019, that they are going to voluntarily send all of their 4,000[65] 737 pilots to have flight simulator time regarding implementation of the MCAS software. The Allied Pilots Association (American Airlines union) does not agree with iPad training on MCAS that is proposed by Boeing in their "fix".[66]

---

[63] Bloomberg, "Former Boeing Engineers Say Relentless Cost-Cutting Sacrificed Safety", Peter Robison, 5/9/2019
[64] Reuters, "Pilots demand better training if Boeing wants to rebuild trust in 737 MAX", Tracy Rucinski, 4/28/2019
[65] The Seattle Times, "FAA could clear Boeing 737 MAX to fly again within weeks", Dominic Gates, 4/26/2019
[66] Investor's Business Daily, "Boeing Faces These 5 EU Demands For 37 Max To Fly Again", Gillian Rich, 7/5/2019

The flight simulator manufacturers were originally given documentation from Boeing, without including information on MCAS software, so no full flight simulator training on the 737 MAX airplanes could happen successfully before June 2019.

Ethiopian Air did purchase a full motion flight simulator just for the 737 MAX 8 airplane. The root problem of no full flight simulator training on MCAS software can be traced directly back to Boeing. Lack of training is not a contributing factor of their crash (ET302). Ethiopian pilots are very well trained, on what Boeing did provide; just not on MCAS.

Having 2 AOA sensors agree before triggering MCAS, displaying them on the glass cockpit, or adding a difference light if they disagreed on the instrument panel, any one of these 3 would force simulator training. Needless to say, none of those things happened as standard features, they can only be added as costly "safety options", with the airlines shouldering the cost of flight simulator training.

Almost all AOA Indicators on previous 737 airplanes are at the extreme edges of the instrument panel. Removing the AOA gages, and not having them displayed on EFIS was a business decision, not a safety decision.

> QUESTION: CAN PILOTS TELL IF THEIR AIRPLANE IS GOING INTO A STALL WITHOUT AOA SENSORS?

The Primary Flight Display (PFD) of EFIS has an Attitude Director Indicator (ADI), which shows aircraft pitch; it is usually about 6" in height and displays pitch ±20°. It would be very easy for a pilot to miss a slow increase of aircraft pitch on the PFD. **AND IT DOES NOTHING TO INDICATE IF THE AIRCRAFT IS _APPROACHING_ A STALL CONDITION.**

Let's reiterate what the ET302 flight crew faced in their brief 5 minutes of flight: try to keep in mind the pilot term "task saturated".

Both flight crews that crashed had many things to react to, in a chaotic situation inside the cockpit, where the pilots didn't have all of the information they needed.

Human Factors – the aircrew was overwhelmed by sights, sounds, and stress which affected how they reacted – because they had no simulator experience with everything that was going to happen, no muscle memory came into play.

Seconds after the Weight on Wheels switch indicated flight, the Captain's Stick Shaker went off causing him to experience severe vibrations of the yoke, along with an irritating loud noise filling the cockpit with about 85 dB of noise.

Having seen the stick shaker go off many times in my past on the ground, it is pretty violent, very hard to hold physically onto the yoke for any amount of time. It not only jerks the yoke back and forth, but it makes a loud noise as well, and that loud noise continued until the end of the flight. (When that noise goes off while when I'm seated in the cockpit doing maintenance, I always pull the speaker circuit breaker first to silence the noise, before attempting to identify what set it off – the sound it generates isn't just loud, it is pretty awful.)

After wheels up, the glass cockpit was immediately full of visible warning annunciations; **ALT DISAGREE**, **AIR SPD DISAGREE**, **MACH TRIM FAIL**, and **SPD TRIM FAIL**. All of the warnings had to be evaluated, the flight crew had to disregard ones that did not apply. (There was no **AOA DISAGREE** warning!) It was the Captain's responsibility to correctly figure out what went wrong, and the actions needed to get his aircraft into a safe condition. He had to eliminate which error messages did not apply and troubleshoot by the seat of his pants whether the horizontal stabilizer, elevators, or an unknown gremlin was causing the problem.

Upon take-off, when flaps were finally retracted, the landing gear lights indicated "gear up", and the take-off speed exceeded 180 knots.

The Captain's AOA sensor indicated a stall. All the conditions to activate MCAS existed, so it took over the moment flaps were fully retracted. It kicked off the autopilot and gave its first *AND* command.

Contributing to the visual collage was the **MASTER CAUTION** indicator/switch illuminating more than once.

Looking at both primary Airspeed Indications, the Captain's had a red barber pole, showing minimum speed tape, whereas the First Officer did not, it was also inaccurate. Not only did the Captain's and First Officer's Airspeed Indicators not agree, neither did their Altimeters.

When they tried to pull back on the yoke it was 4 times as hard, and they didn't know why, since both SMYD Computers were removed.

When they pushed the Pitch Trim thumb switches on the yoke for nose up, the pilots did not push on them long enough to counter MCAS 100%. Every time they did push the thumb switches on the yoke, they reset MCAS. Add to this scenario that every time the pilots lost some pitch to MCAS, the speed of the aircraft increased.

Plus, every time the airplane went pitch down, both pilots would be viewing the ground out of the window in the cockpit. That had to add to the intensity and stress level, the 2 pilots knew they were in a fight for everyone's life aboard the aircraft. The Captain kept his focus, knowing they were barely above the ground, with time very quickly running out, as he tried to keep his aircraft flying with everything he knew (but he wasn't told about MCAS).

As the nose of the aircraft started to pitch down, the aircraft picked up speed, and the aural warning for too much speed went off, affectionately known by pilots as the "clacker" because of the loud irritating sound it makes.

The third aural warning adding onto the cacophony surrounding the pilots was the GPWS announcement of "PULL UP – "PULL UP".

Occasionally the Captain's warning horn would add to the sounds the flight crew had to endure.

One thing we must all agree on, the flight crew complied with the F.A.A. Advisory Circular #2018-23-51, which was issued by the F.A.A. to prevent MCAS from ever causing another crash, it turns out those directions were incomplete. Both of the pilots had memorized the AD guidance. (A brief investigation shortly after the crash revealed that the Aircraft Flight Manual or the Quick Reference Handbook provided by Ethiopian Air did not have that AD inside them.)

Once they removed power to electric STAB TRIM, they tried to move the horizontal stabilizer by using the Pitch Trim Wheel in the cockpit. Unknown to them, it is impossible to do this at high speed. After an attempt to trim the horizontal stabilizer manually, they switched back on STAB TRIM, sealing the planes fate.

All of that happened so quickly, physically, visually, aurally, that entire flight was over in 5 brief minutes, with everything described above (and more). With no flight simulator training on MCAS. Now anyone who reads this and says no pilot needs to train for such a scenario is not telling the truth.

Now you are able to see why I think this flight crew performed valiantly, under the most stressful conditions, while executing everything they were taught. Too bad they had NO simulator training to prepare them for this scenario; the F.A.A. is solely to thank for that decision there.

15. FEDERAL AVIATION ADMINISTRATION

BRIEF HISTORY

Why do we even have the Federal Aviation Administration (F.A.A.)? Two aircraft altered their flight plans so their passengers could do a little sight-seeing while flying over the Grand Canyon, and subsequently had a mid-air collision on 6/30/1956, all 128 people perished in that disaster.

Then on 8/28/1958 the U.S. President signed a bill creating the Civil Aeronautics Authority (C.A.A.). Four months later, 12/31/1958, it began operations. Some of the its objectives were: Air Traffic Control, Accident Investigation, Certification of Aircraft, Inspecting Aviation Maintenance and Manufacturing, Regulating Airports, etc. <u>C.A.A.'s primary mission was to ensure aviation safety.</u>

A few years later, on 4/1/1967, its name was changed to the F.A.A., and investigating transportation accidents was split off to a newly created entity, the National Transportation Safety Board (NTSB).

In today's F.A.A. the primary mission is no longer to "<u>ensure flight safety</u>", it rather "<u>promotes air safety</u>". Funding from Congress no longer allows the F.A.A. the resources to "<u>ensure flight safety</u>."

One of the ways to show how hamstrung the F.A.A. is, they don't have the manpower to analyze pilots reports of safety issues in the NASA database – Aviation Safety Reporting System (ASRS).[67] What this leads to is an inability to identify any national aviation safety trends BEFORE there is an incident or crash.

---

[67] Dallas News, "Several Boeing 737 Max 8 pilots in U.S. complained about suspected safety flaw", Cary Aspinwall, Ariana Giorgi and Dom DiFurio, 3/12/2019

In Europe, there is a different type of government entity, it's only focused on air safety, it's called the European Aviation Safety Agency (EASA).[68]

EASA has stated their conditions before they allow the 737 MAX to fly in Europe:[69]
1. EASA must approve and mandate any design changes by Boeing
2. EASA must complete an additional independent design review
3. 737 MAX flight crews must be "adequately trained"
4. Remedy to Autopilot NOT disengaging in an emergency (new problem???)
5. Fix time lag of FCC microprocessor
6. Solve the problem of the Pitch Trim Wheel being so hard to turn

The acting F.A.A. Administrator, Daniel Elwell, has said the F.A.A. will be the first governmental regulating body to authorize the 737 MAX to fly again.[70]

ODA'S

The F.A.A. has used 14 CFR Part 183 to provide Organization Designation Authorization (ODA) regulations to follow, and they have published F.A.A. Order 8100.15B for their internal policies F.A.A. employees must follow to implement the regulations published in the Federal Register.

---

[68] Forbes, "Airbus Cautious On Regulator And Safety Questions Following Boeing 737 MAX Troubles", Marisa Garcia, 5/21/2019

[69] Investor's Business Daily, "Boeing Faces These 5 EU Demands For 37 Max To Fly Again", Gillian Rich, 7/5/2019

[70] The Seattle Times, "FAA will move first to approve the Boeing 737 MAX to fly again, possibly within weeks", Dominic Gates, 5/24/2019

Nothing in the federal government seems to be easily understood.

Let me try to explain government-ease. Any enforcement document (regulation) must be published first in the Federal Register (public document) and give time for the general population and businesses to comment on the proposed regulations. Once the comment time has expired, then a few weeks or many months elapse before the final regulation is published, after amending it by looking at public comments. When a difficult circumstance arises that may impede a regulation from being implemented, it dies an untimely death, it is never published as a final rule.

Many people (me included) refer to the F.A.A. as the Tombstone Agency. Most of the proposed regulations are written in blood. It takes multiple humans perishing before any real sweeping regulations are published and implemented as a final rule.

The only exemption to this is when the F.A.A. tries to save the federal government from having to expend money. Such are the ODA regulations.

The Organization Designation Authorization (ODA) program is the means by which the FAA grants designee authority for manufacturers (and others) to inspect themselves and certify their products as safe. In essence, removing the cost of oversight onto the companies that previously need certification from the F.A.A.

Federal Government entities have been doing this forever. Having a mind-set that no business will stay alive selling a defective (or deadly) product, it's definitely a Libertarian philosophy. And until the 2 most recent Boeing disasters, worked quite fine in aviation, shifting government costs onto private businesses. But, instead of letting Boeing suffer the consequences of putting profits above consumer safety, the F.A.A., in my opinion, is doing everything it can to keep Boeing selling aircraft and contributing to the U.S. bottom line.

Recently, businesses thought of the ODA regulations as a fast way to bring new products to market, with minimal government oversight. The F.A.A. has oversight on 79 companies it has given this ODA to (as of June 2019). One GAO report back in 2015 estimated that 90% of certifications were done by a single ODA manufacturer.[71] (I'm not certain if this manufacturer was Boeing who certified 90% of their in-house designs, but my educated guess is it is them. Because by 2018 Boeing was certifying 96% of its own work.[72])

Before the ODA's were created, the F.A.A. relied on Designated Engineering Representatives (DER's) for engineering solutions and approved documentation. Small private companies still rely upon DER's for these certifications.

In the past, Boeing paid their DER's. Each DER was approved by the F.A.A., and every year their work was given a robust review before they were allowed to function as a DER the next year. Officials at the F.A.A. had direct supervision over their work at Boeing.

However, it is another ballgame today. Boeing selects their own ODA "team members" and these employees no longer have a business relationship with anyone at the F.A.A.[73] ODA team members approve documentation, but it is submitted to a Boeing manager. Only managers submit documentation to the F.A.A., as well as hiring and firing all the staff on the ODA "team".

Managers can limit safety analysis, safety testing, etc., to meet schedules and avoid cost overruns. They are able to force subordinates to bend to their will, if employees want to keep their jobs and retirement

---

[71] D.O.T. I.G. Audit Report #AV-2016-001, "FAA Lacks an Effective Staffing Model and Risk-Based Oversight Process for Organization Designation Authorization", 10/15/2015

[72] New York Time, "The Roots of Boeing's 737 MAX Crisis: A Regulator Relaxes Its Oversight", Natalie Kitroeff, David Gelles and Jack Nicas, 7/27/2019

[73] The Seattle Times, "Engineers say Boeing pushed to limit safety testing in race to certify planes, including 737 MAX", Dominic Gates and Mike Baker, 5/5/2019

package. Don't get the impression that Boeing disregards safety, they don't, but employees on the floor must ask themselves if a safety issue arises, if it's important enough to lose their jobs over – before they speak up.

At Boeing it is no longer safety first. Profits are now the focus of the company, that and increasing their stock price. Safety is always considered; it is just not the driving force behind Boeing as it once was.

BOEING OVERSIGHT

Of the 79 entities that have been granted by the F.A.A. their own ODA status, only Boeing has a dedicated F.A.A. office to oversee just them.

Ali Bahrami, F.A.A. Associate Administrator, in charge of aviation safety, is pushing for even less oversight of aircraft manufacturing. Back in 2012, he chaired a committee of aviation professionals, and now wants Certified Design Organization (CDO). In this utopian future, there will be no ODA's who submit paperwork to the F.A.A.; people working in aircraft manufacturing will completely self-certify aircraft design, without oversight from the F.A.A..[74]

Mr. Bahrami has another distinction that is part of his resume, he was the F.A.A. office manager who oversaw a stable of engineers (20-25 employees) responsible for certifying all new airplanes from Boeing. However, when the Department of Transportation I.G. investigated his office in 2012, they found safety engineers who feared retaliation from Mr. Bahrami because they were trying to hold Boeing to be accountable.[75] During this time period the 737 MAX was being created

---

[74] The Seattle Times, "Engineers say Boeing pushed to limit safety testing in race to certify planes, including 737 MAX", Dominic Gates and Mike Baker, 5/5/2019

[75] The Seattle Times, "With close industry ties, FAA safety chief pushed more delegation of oversight to Boeing", Dominic Gates, 4/14/2019

and certified; Boeing had a working flight simulator that looked exactly like the cockpit of those being built today.

On Wednesday, 7/31/2019, Mr. Bahrami testified in front of U.S. Senators and admitted that he personally overrode decisions of F.A.A. safety engineers to let 737 MAX production continue.[76]

Boeing's oversight office is located near the final manufacturing process, in Washington State (Renton, WA).

It is my personal opinion that the Boeing oversight office of the F.A.A. is understaffed, overwhelmed, and inexperienced; a total of 40 employees are assigned there, but after counting admin staff, only 20-25 employees actually oversee Boeing. When you consider that Boeing has a staff of 40,000 engineers spread across America and foreign vendors, this is a pitiful number for oversight responsibilities of such a sprawling nationwide corporation.

F.A.A. MANAGEMENT – APPROVING DOCUMENTATION

Back on 3/8/2017 the F.A.A. granted Boeing's 737 MAX a Derivative Type Certificate (also called an Amended Type Certificate) based on the original 737 Type Certificate. It is against Federal Air Regulations for two types of aircraft to share a Type Certificate if they handle differently. Without MCAS software, both aircraft types do handle differently. MCAS is going to fail, as all avionics fail – then how does a pilot fly an aircraft that he/she is rated for, but has no experience hand flying it?

Giving a Derivative Type Certificate to the 737 MAX is just one of the things the F.A.A. did wrong.

---

[76] PBS News Hour, "Senators clash with FAA officials over Boeing Max oversight", 7/31/2019

Next on the F.A.A. greatest hits list is they prepared a 30-page document, noting every little thing different between 737's before granting the Derivative Type Certificate. However, MCAS did not make it onto a single page of the differences document.[77]

There are two documents normally within reach of each pilot in the cockpit. The first is the Aircraft Flight Manual (AFM), where the manufacturer documents every system in the aircraft, and how it works. For the 737 MAX this document is over 1,400 pages.

Another document in a commercial aircraft cockpit will be the Quick Reference Handbook (QRH). It includes a handy way for pilots to find information on any system they use to fly the aircraft. Inside this document are the Abnormal / Emergency Checklists. In the 737 MAX, this document is over 300 pages.

A former F.A.A. employee, Mark Forkner, was Boeing's chief **Technical** pilot for the 737 MAX (Ed Wilson was Boeing's last chief **Test** pilot on the 737 MAX). Mr. Forkner "flew" the 737 MAX only on a stationary simulator, which at the time did not fully simulate MCAS software. Before Boeing did a cost restructure of their company in 2009[78], technical pilots actually flew in the aircraft they were supposed to be the experts on.

A request was made from one former F.A.A. official (Mr. Forkner) to other F.A.A. officials to remove any mention of MCAS from the AFM.[79] Needless to say current F.A.A. officials honored a request from a former F.A.A. official. (That's why the term MCAS is in the acronym section of the AFM, but not in the actual document – it wasn't

---

[77] The Verge, "The many human errors that brought down the Boeing 737 Max", Darryl Campbell, 5/2/2019

[78] Axios, "Report: Boeing test pilots 'had no real input' in final development of MCAS system", Gigi Sukin, 5/3/2019

[79] New York Times, "Boeing Built Deadly Assumptions Into 737 MAX, Blind to a Late Design Change", Jack Nicas, Natalie Kitroeff, David Gelles, and James Glanz, 6/1/2019

completely purged when the F.A.A. had Boeing remove MCAS references.)

Both of the aforementioned documents (AFM and QRH) require one person's signature from the F.A.A. authorizing their use. Boeing wrote both documents, but the F.A.A. has to approve them. Not only is Boeing negligent for not including a description of MCAS, but at least one person employed by the F.A.A. is culpable as well for this negligence.

Read Paragraph **"F."** of this chapter titled "<u>SLEEPING WITH BOEING</u>?"; it paints a picture of a federal agency so in tuned with those it oversees that they don't either read the documentation or can't comprehend what's missing. In either case, they act as an arm of the company they are supposed to watch over.

Why do I accuse the F.A.A. of collusion with Boeing? Because if changes were made to either document, such as describing MCAS in the AFM, or adding an Emergency Checklist for MCAS in the QRH, the results would require full flight simulator training. Remember how no full flight simulator training was one of Boeing's biggest selling points for the 737 MAX?

What the F.A.A. did on approving 737 MAX documentation is a case of criminal negligence, leading to the deaths of 346 people. Prosecutors from Illinois and Washington need to investigate and take action.

F.A.A. MANAGEMENT – INACTION

Let's take it for granted that the F.A.A. blew it on the certification of the 737 MAX.

Let's highlight a different aspect of the F.A.A. here, inability to act when confronting a serious action that will cost **BILLIONS** to the company they oversee.

After the first crash of JT610, F.A.A. Airworthiness Safety Inspectors (ASI's) for Southwest Airlines found out about the lack of an AOA DISAGREE warning on the 737 MAX. They managed Southwest Airlines operating certificate and considered grounding the fleet of 737 MAX aircraft at Southwest. When management at Southwest were informed, they insisted that Boeing modify their 737 MAX aircraft so the AOA DISAGREE warning would be displayed on their pilot's PFD.

Because of Southwest Airlines management's reaction, making the software problem moot by installing the "safety package", the F.A.A. ASI's let the matter drop, concluding that emergency action was not required.

As pointed out by Jon Weaks, Southwest's union president, the AOA DISAGREE warning was written about in their 737 MAX Aircraft Flight Manuals, but not working on their aircraft.[80]

Now imagine if the consensus at the F.A.A. was to have the flying public's safety as their primary mission, and not encouraging the aviation business, what would have happened? Could Southwest's Inspectors have told other F.A.A. certificate management offices about the missing warning alert on their 737 MAX operators, like American Airlines or United?

F.A.A. MANAGEMENT BAD DECISONS

---

[80] Wall Street Journal, "Boeing Didn't Advise Airlines, FAA That It Shut Off Warning System", Andy Pasztor, 5/29/2019

Being a former F.A.A. employee, I do understand pressures put on the governmental civilian workforce to get results in a timely period. But there were times I had to stop airplanes from flying, because the aircraft wanting to be flown by pilots to complete their Flight Check mission were not airworthy. Safety should always come first.

Not a single F.A.A. employee stood up and said that there had been a minimum of 80 AOA failures/problems in 15 years. When a system is classified like MCAS was supposed to be, then that system can only have a 1 in 1,000,000,000 chance of failure. Some government civil servant should have known there were on average at least 5 AOA failures every year who could have raised the alarm before MCAS was finalized.

"Statistics can lie, and statisticians are liars" was a phrase I heard many times in my undergraduate Statistics Course at the University of Michigan (which I did pass). One good example is when Boeing's CEO says air travel is so safe in the U.S., there has been but one fatality in 10 years, 7 billion passengers traveled safely on 90 million flights in the last decade. Turn that around and say: worldwide fatalities on all 737 MAX flights amounts to only 1 death for every 300,000 passengers flown. (Hmmm… I'd play the Mega Millions lottery if my odds of "winning" were 1 in 300,000, wouldn't you?)

On any given day, a very conservative estimate is that there are approximately 26,000 commercial passenger flights in the U.S. Given 365 days in a year, that roughly amounts to 10,000,000 flights a year. Dividing that number for 15 years by the 80 AOA malfunctions yields a failure rate of 1 in 1.8 million flights, well above what a critical safety of flight system should have.

This is not Monday morning "quarterbacking", this is protecting lives; it should be the primary responsibility of the F.A.A. (it's not).

Three unions filed a 2/2017 report on safety issues that could potentially cause a 737 MAX airplane crash, that F.A.A. management recognized as true, but signed off on them anyways, to keep to Boeing's schedule to launch the 737 MAX aircraft. Here are just 3 of the remaining safety issues:[81]

1. Insufficient fireproofing around the Auxiliary Power Unit (APU) in the tail of airplane (APU is a jet engine used to power electrical circuits while the 737 MAX airplane is on the ground, think of it a 100KW generator in the tail)
2. Incorrect wiring inside the fuel tanks (high voltage / current to switches internal to the fuel tanks)
3. Rudder cables were unprotected if a LEAP 1B engine came apart in flight

So not only does MCAS software have multiple problems, but these 3 other issues are still unresolved in the 737 MAX. A minor note, this report was filed one month before the F.A.A. certified the 737 MAX as airworthy, although the F.A.A. could have acted, they instead chose to greenlight the aircraft with known airworthy problems.

On May 15, 2019, acting F.A.A. Administrator Daniel K. Elwell stated before a House Committee that he personally thinks that MCAS is a safety critical system.[82] Yet later in his testimony he emphasized that his agency's position is MCAS did not cause a safety issue. (The absolute top guy in the F.A.A. twists himself in knots to defend Boeing? for what? And then how are other people below him to take a stand on safety?)

F.A.A. has understaffed its certification office that oversees Boeing. With 20 - 25 F.A.A. employees providing oversight on 950

---

[81] The Seattle Times, "Engineers say Boeing pushed to limit safety testing in race to certify planes, including 737 MAX", Dominic Gates and Mike Baker, 5/5/2019

[82] Yahoo Finance, "The FAA expects Boeing's 737 MAX 8 application next week", Alexis Keenen, 5/15/2019

Boeing AR's,[83] it is just not enough. That roughly equates to one F.A.A. inspector/engineer looking over the paperwork generated by 38 Boeing inspectors (AR's) out of 950 who oversee 130,000 employee's work. Logically, there are not enough hours in the day to do that. Carrying that out, each F.A.A. inspector can dedicate about 10 minutes a day each week for every individual AR they oversee, along with their other duties.

Boeing inspector's (AR's) work hard but don't build relationships with people overseeing them at the F.A.A. Remember, only Boeing managers actually submit paperwork to the F.A.A. for oversight, there is very little interaction between the F.A.A. oversight personnel and Boeing's AR employees on the floor. And when someone from the F.A.A. does physically visit either Boeing or one of their 900 vendors on the 737 MAX, the majority of their time is spent reviewing paperwork, not interacting with AR's on the floor. Currently the F.A.A. is aiming at performing just the minimum inspections, and they are failing at that very low goal they set for themselves.

Back in February 2016, EASA put a certification document online that stated in certain conditions (flaps retracted, speed above 230 knots) 737 MAX pilots will need to manipulate the Pitch Trim Wheel to move the horizontal stabilizer.[84] Some people speculate that EASA knew about the MCAS problem and publishing this paper would help European pilots fly the 737 MAX.

THINK ABOUT IT:

Why was this MCAS information not included in the Aircraft Flight Manual?

---

[83] The Seattle Times, "With close industry ties, FAA safety chief pushed more delegation of oversight to Boeing", Dominic Gates, 4/14/2019

[84] Reuters, "INSIGHT – Regulators knew before crashes that 737 MAX control was confusing in some conditions", Jamie Freed, 3/31/2019

Why was the EASA document not incorporated into the differences training on the 56-minute iPad training course?

The F.A.A. issued an initial Airworthiness Directive (AD) #2018-23-51 without knowing all the particulars of MCAS software capabilities – it's not what the F.A.A. did in the past, when it was the Gold Standard for the world to see, when F.A.A. management was both competent and educated in the systems it had oversight on.

SLEEPING WITH BOEING?

My personal experience can explain how F.A.A. Inspectors can be influenced in regard to the airlines (and manufacturers) they are supposed to have oversight of.

A long, long time ago, (past the statute of limitations), I was Temporary Duty Away from Station (TDY), assigned to a F.A.A. Flight Standard District Office in the Midwest. My role was as an F.A.A. Avionics Airworthiness Safety Inspector.

There was a whole team of Airworthiness Safety Inspectors that went to the site of a major airline, now defunct. During the on-site inspection the entire team was invited to go on a yacht, where there would be free booze, and every single person was offered a female companion. (Back then, females were rarely part of most inspection teams; all of us in this group were males.)

Not being a perfect person, I did think about it before I declined. In my opinion it was not illegal, just immoral (I was married at the time), along with being wrong ethically. They left me the rental car while all of the others partook of the invitation.

Way back then, this was called being in bed with the operator (management of the airline).

When looking at how F.A.A. management has allowed Boeing to have the keys to the kingdom – certifying themselves without proper oversight, I'm wondering if the people in my old inspection team didn't retire like me, but just moved to Seattle (kidding).

F.A.A. convened a Flight Standardization Board (FSB) comprised of experts inside the F.A.A. who were supposed to be currently certified and trained Airworthiness Safety Inspectors. These people determined the training requirements for the 737 MAX. When a whistleblower testified about this FSB, it was about the people on the FSB who determined that pilots didn't need full flight simulator training. Even the F.A.A. Administrator indirectly admitted the staff, i.e., engineers and managers, did not have current certifications.[85]

In actuality, the FSB is really composed of ASI's, pilots, engineers, and other experts. But eventually a manager makes the final decision if there is a disagreement among board members.

That may seem shocking, but it is fairly typical in my personal experience, having been an F.A.A. employee for 25 years. Supervisors and Managers in the F.A.A. do not need current certifications, because they manage people, and are not supposed to be involved in the nuts and bolts of technical matters; at least that is the general philosophy of the F.A.A., before I retired.

Specifically, it was the support staff, i.e., engineers, who did not have the appropriate credentials, nor up-to-date training to perform the duties to support the FSB. I also suspect the person in charge of running the FSB was a manager (Stacy Klein) who did not have current certifications or training to perform this task at the time.

What were the results of the FSB? No additional training would be required of pilots, other than watching what boiled down to a 56-minute tutorial on an iPad, on differences training for the 737 MAX 8.

---

[85] Wall Street Journal, "FAA Disputes Allegations of Lapses on 737 MAX Training", Andy Pasztor, 4/5/2019

That group of individuals in the FSB determined no level "D" flight simulator training (full motion) was required after MCAS was invented and then installed into the 737 MAX.

One fact in both crashes proves how wrong they were… both flight crews were so distracted by what was happening in the cockpit, they both crashed. They had no preparation for such an intense scenario in a 737 MAX full motion flight simulator.

Earlier I detailed how the F.A.A. came up with a plan to eliminate government employees from the payroll, and have private companies pay their own inspectors to police themselves; it's called ODA (Organization Designation Authorization).

To defend this practice, the acting F.A.A. Administrator was called in front of a Senate Sub-Committee hearing on March 27, 2019. At that time, he stated the F.A.A. would need a workforce of an additional 10,000 employees, with a cost of $1.8 billion a year to do proper oversight.[86] Of course, it was agreed that was too much, so the status quo continues to this day. (No one called out the figures quoted are 100% inaccurate.)

> QUESTION: IF BOEING HAS ONLY 950 AR INSPECTORS, WHY WOULD THE F.A.A. NEED 10,000 MORE MANUFACTURING ASI'S?

Over my career, I've heard the F.A.A. make false and inaccurate statements, regardless of whomever is the U.S. President. The F.A.A. even has a book, that management employees can look up to find the "canned" response, so the agency does not look bad, based on any truth they can ferret out in the Congressional request being made.

---

[86] The Seattle Times, "Engineers say Boeing pushed to limit safety testing in race to certify planes, including 737 MAX", Dominic Gates and Mike Baker, 5/5/2019

One of the problems the F.A.A. is dealing with is paying people enough to perform government service. They cannot keep up with the private sector, so they do not hire the best and brightest as they did in the past. So current decisions are made by persons whose intelligence can be questioned. Disparity in pay has been going on for a long time, it has surpassed the "Peter Principle" and the management in the F.A.A. are not the scholars they once were.

Besides current F.A.A. management lacking updated qualifications and intelligence, their engineers are not equal to those in the private sector. Good engineers in the private sector can command pay above $200,000, whereas, in the F.A.A. they are paid half as much. Congress is even debating to curtail the current civil service retirement system (FERS), the only thing that may lure adequate engineers who may trade immediate salary requirements for job security. (Future employees are questioning civil service job security after the 35-day government shut-down. Even more disconcerting is Congress wants to change the current FERS retirement system because it is too generous, a retirement plan that became effective in 1987.)

16. MCAS - FLAWS

There are so many flaws in MCAS, I don't think the system can be saved without significant improvements.

MCAS is not fault tolerant, relying only on the AOA sensors.

MCAS has no redundancy, only one FCC is active at a time.

<u>Boeing did not comply with 14 CFR 25.1309 "Equipment, Systems, and Installations"</u>.

That specific federal regulation describes various conditions for all safety of flight equipment (hardware or software). Any failure condition that prevents the safe flight and landing are extremely improbable (read "catastrophic" or "critical", i.e., once in 1,000,000,000 flight hours). Systems warnings must be designed to minimize crew errors that could create additional hazards. An analysis of all possible modes of failure, "**including malfunctions and damage from external sources**", through either simulator or flight testing. Flight crew must be able to detect faults.

A separate issue is having only 2 AOA sensors to trigger MCAS software; no fault tolerance. If both sensors disagree, which one is correct? Without another system input, MCAS has a single point of failure, the AOA sensors. MCAS no longer gets an input from the "g" – force sensors in the ADIRU's, even though it is critical to have more than one point of failure for critical flight safety equipment.

Besides MCAS not being fault tolerant, there is no redundancy. For someone thinking that using both AOA sensors makes MCAS a redundant system, they would be wrong. Redundancy requires two SYSTEMS, not two identical sensors.

To have true redundancy means that two systems must be identical and switchable when there is a failure. Illustrating my point is the airplane autopilot system, in the 737 MAX there are two identical autopilot systems and if one fails then the pilots switch to the other one. When MCAS fails, it either has to automatically switch to the inactive FCC or allow the pilots to switch to the good one manually. From what I understand if the FCC stops working completely, then the other FCC will take its place automatically. But, what if only the MCAS software portion of the FCC acts erratically?

Collins Aerospace failed to write MCAS software in accordance with known civilian aviation standards, that is evident in the results. (Collins may have used a military software standard, since they do so much D.O.D sub-contracting.) Two patches to flight critical software within 24 months of being released should never have occurred if the software was executed flawlessly, as all catastrophic system safety software should be.

There is no indicator in the cockpit to tell pilots when MCAS software is operating correctly. (It should be green in color – not a caution or warning, just information on a system that is working properly.)

I am not familiar enough with MCAS operations to know if it has a MCAS FAIL warning when it, or any associated system giving inputs to it malfunctions.

Since the first Boeing 737 MAX delivery, and for the next 2 years, there was no AOA DISAGREE warning on 80% of the fleet, but Boeing kept it secret for over a year. What other problems does Boeing currently know about, but is not telling anyone about?

On the pilot's PFD there is no AOA Indicator, in contrast to what the NTSB has been recommending for years.[87]

---

[87] Boeing, Aerospace Magazine #12, "Angle of Attack Story", Brian D. Kelley

All of the required systems needed for MCAS software to function have to be removed from the Minimum Equipment List. The unstable 737 MAX should never be dispatched for flight with revenue paying passengers on-board without everything MCAS needs being 100% functional.

Disabling MCAS does not fix the stall problem inherent in the design of the 737 MAX 8 !!!

Keeping MCAS is also problematic, as any future problems (including intermittent malfunctions) will endanger crew and passengers.

17. BOEING'S PRELIMINARY FIX

As of May 23, 2019, Boeing has a software fix, and has flown a 737 MAX 8 on 207 flights for a total of 360 flight hours testing it;[88] they just have not submitted it to the F.A.A. for final approval yet.

The F.A.A. convened another FSB, that determined what the minimum future training would be for the 737 MAX[89], even before the software update was formally submitted (it's a 30-minute iPad training module). I know, because the F.A.A. published it, and I responded with a comment that it was very premature to state the training requirements would not require full motion flight simulator training on the 737 MAX, before a final fix was officially approved.

From what I've been able to glean so far is a fix to MCAS software, version 12.1:
- ▶ MCAS only kicks in once, until the next time a stall is detected
- ▶ MCAS will not activate if there is a 5.5° degree difference between AOA sensors
- ▶ AOA DISAGREE warning will be enabled on all aircraft (if disagree 10° for 10 sec.)
- ▶ Warn light **may** be installed (AOA sensor difference of more than 5.5° illuminates it)
- ▶ MCAS force applied to the yoke is same as the pilots can apply
- ▶ *Additional training needed*:
  FSB – an additional 30-minute DVD / iPad lesson on MCAS

It will be up to the F.A.A. and Boeing to sell the above ideas to the rest of the countries who have ordered the 737 MAX 8.

---

[88] Investor's Business Daily, "EU Makes These 3 Demands on Boeing 737 Max As Top Airline Backs Plane, Gillian Rich, 5/22/2019

[89] Aviation Daily, "FAA OK's Updated MCAS for 737 MAX, Awaits Industry Comments", Nick Zazulia, 4/17/2019

When, or if, the F.A.A. approves all of the changes, then they will issue an Airworthiness Directive, a mandatory compliance document. Hopefully they will include directions for maintenance, besides how to load software. It would be really good to have maintenance perform a test of all of the AOA sensors on every 737 MAX, to see if they are all starting from the same baseline, since two have already failed.

It appears the regulators have not considered everything.

Thinking MCAS is fixed, and take-off crashes will never happen again, is not very realistic. Will every single FCC unit, in stock or currently in shipment, have the updated software? In my experience one or two always slip through, even though avionics technicians are supposed to verify the software level of every unit to be installed, before putting it into an aircraft, not everyone does. (Human Factors)

Another situation has not been adequately covered as well. If upon take-off, MCAS is disabled because of a disparity between AOA sensors, then sometime during the cruise portion of that flight it has the autopilot fail, the exact scenario why MCAS was invented will occur, there will be another aircraft crash attributed to MCAS. Only this time the aircraft crash will occur due to loss of lift during cruise, with all lives lost, aircraft obliterated, and possible loss of life to people on the ground.

What happens if there is an intermittent problem occurring on one of the other inputs to MCAS, it could engage repeatedly and mimic the crashes of JT610 and ET302.

After two proven aircraft crashes where everyone lost their lives, and both airframes were destroyed within 132 calendar days, it would indicate the F.A.A. needs to perform another System Safety Analysis on 737 MAX MCAS software.

Even as I write this first volume on the deadly 737 MAX airplanes, another shoe has dropped on Boeing's plans to return the 737 MAX to service.

Boeing delivered in the middle of May 2019, a completed software update to the FCC that was to rectify the flawed MCAS software.[90] Pilots from the F.A.A. are testing it on the 737 MAX stationary flight simulator that Boeing owns in Seattle. Overseeing these tests are members from the Technical Advisory Board (TAB) which was assembled by the F.A.A. as another way to have more experts observe the software update of MCAS.[91]

While performing an expanded series of tests, trying to uncover all flight conditions MCAS would activate in, something happened in June 2019. While performing the Runaway Stabilizer Abnormal Checklist, the horizontal stabilizer did not have adequate response time from the pilots moving the Pitch Trim thumb switches on the yoke.[92]

In the flight simulator F.A.A. test pilots were performing certification tests of the FCC, flooding it with simulated bad data, when it commanded the horizontal stabilizer to force the "aircraft" into a hard nose down.[93] Supposedly it is unrelated to MCAS.

The most damning aspect of this new development, is Boeing knew of this exact condition, experienced it in their certification tests, and their AR's certified it anyway.

QUESTION: HOW IMPORTANT IS A RUNAWAY TRIM PROCEDURE?

---

[90] The Seattle Times, "Boeing says its software fix for the 737 MAX is ready, awaits FAA approval", Dominic Gates and Mike Baker, 5/16/2019

[91] Bloomberg, "Boeing Needs Up to Three Months to Fix Latest 737 Max Problem", Alan Levin, Julie Johnsson and Shaun Courtney, 6/27/2019

[92] Wall Street Journal, "Boeing 737 MAX Likely Grounded Until Late This Year", Andy Pasztor and Andrew Tangel, 6/27/2019

[93] Bloomberg, "Latest 737 Max Fault That Alarmed Test Pilots Rooted in Software", Alan Levin, 7/27/2019

Simulating Runaway Trim in a 737 MAX airplane mock-up is relatively easy, recovery, not so much. Looking at the situation where a horizontal stabilizer is trying to go pitch down from a level flight profile can take a little less than 20 seconds from a straight and level flight condition to a full nose down dive. When a pilot moves the Pitch Trim thumb switches to command nose up, he/she is expecting an almost immediate effect.

Once in a dive the 737 MAX picks up speed quickly, if done at cruise speeds and altitude, moving the Pitch Trim Wheel becomes physically impossible after a few seconds.

General Aviation airplanes that have Pitch Trim installed usually use two relays to connect a DC voltage driving a motor, and almost immediately after touching the thumb wheel switches the much smaller sized horizontal stabilizer will move in either direction.

Inside the FCC, completely separated from MCAS software, is a program running on a CPU that calculates how much movement speed should be signaled to the horizontal stabilizer's electric motor. Speed and altitude affect the speed at which the FCC will drive the electric motor attached to the jackscrew that physically moves the horizontal stabilizer. (A software sub-routine calculates how much drive signal it should send to the STAB TRIM electric motor.)

The F.A.A. labels this as a "potential risk" in public statements. Privately, one F.A.A. engineer considered this new problem as "catastrophic".[94]

Initial findings are that one of the microprocessors (CPU) inside the FCC is not dispensing the data fast enough to be converted into significant movement of the horizontal stabilizer quickly enough.[95] So,

---

[94] CNBC – Interview, Host was Andrew Sorkin and the guest was Carter Copeland, 6/28/2019

[95] New York Times, "Boeing's 737 Max Suffers Setback in Flight Simulator Test",

when the 737 MAX is out of trim, nose pointed down, the FCC was given input from the thumb switches on the yoke to pull up, but there was a noticeable lag time between when the manual commands were made and the time the horizontal stabilizer moved.[96]

Before I analyze this software glitch, please take a moment to understand how this newest software problem was discovered by Boeing's engineers who self-certified this kludge of software patches in 2017. What other decisions did Boeing engineers make to meet the deadline for delivery? Why would Boeing engineers overlook a significant delay from when the pilots ask for horizontal stabilizer movement by moving thumb wheel switches, and when the it actually moves up or down?[97]

Boeing has stated this problem may be taken care of by simply re-writing the program, essentially speeding up the software, and it might take 3 months.

Outside experts think Boeing is going to have to replace one CPU, then it might take 6 months to have MCAS functioning correctly. (I'm an expert in general avionics, and I'll bet my personal SUV title against anyone putting up a running Chevy corvette title, that it'll be around Christmas time of 2020 before a 737 MAX flies again, if they have to replace a CPU.)

First, let me explain the software problem of not processing code fast enough. When Boeing designed the 737 MAX, they removed the Stall Management / Yaw Damper Computer unit and placed all of its software functions into an existing FCC unit. (Kind of like putting 10 gallons of feces into a 5-gallon cowboy hat, you can pour it all in, but some of it isn't going to fit too comfortably inside.)

Natalie Kitroeff and Tiffany Hsu, 6/26/2019
[96] Forbes, " 'Runaway Stabilizer Condition' Could Delay Boeing 737 MAX's Return To 2020", Peter Cohen, 6/28/2019
[97] Reuters, "U.S. regulator cites new flaw on grounded Boeing 737 MAX", David Shepardson and Eric M. Johnson, 6/26/2019

Try and think about processing a ton more data but doing it on an ancient CPU.

Boeing is going to find out that giving a higher priority in software to process the manual commands from the Pitch Trim thumb wheel switches, another critical function must be dropped to a lower priority. Boeing will have to make a Sophie's Choice, what critical safety function do they slow down, to speed up the software causing the current problem?

Boeing can dream of extra processing cycles, but they have too many sub-routines running on a slow processor. One of the government's software engineers assigned to this testing does not believe Boeing can do something about increasing the response speed and not have the law of unintended consequences prevail with disastrous results in another CPU function.

Rockwell Collins stated it took them 3 years to do the overall design, build the hardware, and write the software code for the Boeing FCC inside the 737 MAX. If Collins cut no corners like Boeing did when they reused the tired old platform of the 737 to manufacture an airplane that crashed twice in 132 days, then it may only rise to a low panic level. If software can correct this latest problem.

If Collins cut corners and used existing hardware, they already had on the shelf to speed up delivery of the new and improved FCC, like reusing an Intel 80286 CPU, it could be years before the 737 MAX sees the sky again.

Airbus used the Intel 80286 CPU in their first version of the A320 which was certified in 1986, and earlier versions of Boeing's 737 NG did too! (Intel started selling 80286 CPU's in 1982.)

Going back to the 1980's I owned a screaming fast 286 desktop computer (a real improvement over the 8080 CPU). What a beast, executing 16 bit commands at a blazing clock speed of 8 MHz, maximum RAM was an astounding 16 MB, it even had a 20MB hard drive – so much capacity, it was unfillable back then. My friend bought one from a Radio Shack employee for $2,000 in 1988.

Again, having 40 years of experience in avionics, I know something about building avionics equipment. No manufacturer ever chooses the latest and greatest CPU to run their new software code, too many future headaches to anticipate. In almost every case they choose a CPU that has been tested across multiple industries for at least two years and has zero problems.

Figure in when the first production FCC was turned out; Boeing had a stationary simulator in Seattle by 2012 that had 2 production FCC units in it. Calculating back 3 years to 2009, when the design of hardware was pretty much finalized, then the CPU would at best be from the 2007-2008 time period.

A scary worst-case scenario of requiring a new CPU will require a new "motherboard" (hardware), it doesn't put Boeing back to square one, but I cannot conceive of anything less than a year delay, AFTER a decision is made from their Board of Directors to proceed with such drastic hardware changes.

Don't forget there are 2 CPU's inside both of the FCC's,[98] and they run similar programs at the same time, one is from Intel, the other CPU is from AMD. My assumption is they run at very similar clock speeds. If one is replaced, then the other CPU will have to be changed as well. Any hardware fix to this software program problem is going to more complex than most people can visualize.

Even fixing MCAS software is complicated. One group of software developers are assigned to the Intel CPU, and a different group of programmers should be assigned to the AMD processor. If one group

---

[98] Website, "737 MCAS – Failure is an Option", Peter Lemme, 11/15/2018

programs a flaw into the code a single processor, the other group being separated, will not likely make the same mistake.

In addition to a slower than expected manual pitch trim command is the scenario the F.A.A. test pilots used to create the Runaway Trim. Certain bits (ones and zeros) were swapped inside the microprocessor (CPU), those bits are used to assess current flight conditions and movements of the control surfaces.[99] Basically, one bit told the CPU that MCAS was engaged, the other bit commanded full nose down of the horizontal stabilizer, and it was "off-to-the-races". (Boeing was supposed to test for these scenarios BEFORE Boeing self-certified it safe for flight!)

Of the 3 pilots chosen by the F.A.A. to fly a simulator with 33 different situations that are theoretically possible for the 737 MAX to encounter over its lifespan, 2 responded in time. A third pilot was not so lucky,[100] after approximately 16 seconds, the simulators nose was pointing down and its airspeed was above 400 knots – the simulation was then abruptly ended.[101]

Because a qualified U.S. airline pilot could not recover the 737 MAX, Boeing has decided to change its software architecture in the FCC.[102]

A proposed change is to have both FCC's active at the same time. Besides monitoring both AOA sensors for any discrepancies, the FCC's will also compare airspeeds and altitudes.[103]

---

[99] The Seattle Times, "Newly stringent FAA tests spur a fundamental software redesign of Boeing's 737 MAX flight controls", Dominic Gates, 8/1/2019
[100] New York times, "Boeing's 737 MAX Suffers Setback in Flight Simulator Test", Natalie Kitroeff and Tiffany Hsu, 6/26/2019
[101] Wall Street Journal, "737 MAX Safety Tests Covering Increasingly Remote Failure Risks", Andy Pasztor, 8/2/2019
[102] Reuters, "Boeing to change 737 MAX flight control software to address flaw: sources", David Shepardson and Eric M. Johnson, 8/1/2019
[103] Bloomberg, "Boeing Redesigning 737 Max Flight Controls to Boost Reliability", Julie Johnsson, 8/1/2019

18. A REAL FIX

MORE THAN A SINGLE POINT OF FAILURE

Originally MCAS on the 737 MAX was designed to accept two separate inputs before it activated, AOA sensor and "g" force input. Early on Boeing dropped the "g" force input and relied only on an AOA sensor.

It does not matter if the 737 MAX uses one or two AOA sensors, that is a single point of failure. If either one of the two AOA sensors malfunctions, which one is correct? MCAS in that scenario has zero input for stall detection.

To make this point perfectly clear, relying on just two identical AOA sensors, one on each side of the airplane to trigger MCAS is problematic. If there is no failure from either sensor, MCAS works as advertised. If one of the 2 sensors fail, then MCAS cannot activate.

I labor on the above point so much because it is critical the reader understand that MCAS relying on a single AOA sensor caused both aircraft to crash.

Adding a third AOA sensor would allow MCAS to pick the 2 that agree and carry on functioning normally.

Boeing is resisting this decision because all of their other commercial airplanes rely on just two AOA sensors, and this could trigger a backlash from current customers to add a third sensor on existing Boeing airplanes.

Adding that 3rd AOA sensor is required if Boeing wants to make MCAS safe and operational even if one AOA sensor malfunctions. An alternative is to use an avionics box that already is present on the 737 MAX; the ADIRU's have 3 accelerometers that sense motion in three dimensions (3-D).

Technology exists to use the 'g" forces that the accelerometers sense and write software code to not only sense the pitch of the aircraft, but how it is reacting to outside forces – winds aloft. These ADIRU's already calculate lateral winds aloft, it may not be a simple code to write, but definitely possible to have them calculate vertical winds aloft and their direction.

Airbus has three AOA sensors, as should the 737 MAX, since this a single point of failure (AOA sensors). If the either one of the two AOA sensors fails on a 737 MAX, how is a pilot to determine which one is correct? If there are three AOA sensors, a pilot can visually observe the two that agree, as would MCAS software.

I've helped to install a new antenna on a pressurized aircraft numerous times. Antennas need a "doubler" (metal plate larger than the new antenna's base) to strengthen the aircraft skin, which mounts the antenna slightly higher from the exterior structure of the aircraft.

AOA sensors rely on being flush to the skin of the aircraft to determine airflow being measured by the nose of the aircraft. Boeing engineers could mount a third AOA sensor, flush with the skin by modifying the inside structure of the 737 MAX airplane to be stronger. Having worked on 737's, I know there is plenty of room in the nose of the aircraft to accomplish this.

Having read plenty of crash reports, someone will point out that even though Airbus A320's have three AOA sensors, one still crashed because two AOA sensors failed. Anyone who makes this argument doesn't know anything about that specific crash.

Read the following account of an Airbus that had three AOA sensors, but still crashed after relying on the two that agreed – but were frozen in a bad position.

An Airbus A320-200 crashed on November 27, 2008, killing all 7 on board near Perpignan, France. The people who perished: 2 pilots flying the A320 registered as D-AXLA, plus a Captain and three engineers from New Zeeland Air, and a representative from New Zeeland C.A.A..[104]

Before its final flight, it had been flown to be repainted in the new operator's color-scheme, Air New Zeeland. During the paint stripping process the three AOA sensors were not protected, and water penetrated one of the AOA sensors housing on each side of the aircraft (probably during the pressure washing, before painting). The third AOA sensor that water did not penetrate was probably the one located higher and further back than the others.

When all maintenance had been performed, a Captain from Air New Zeeland was aboard, to monitor the test flight (no revenue passengers were on board). He requested the aircraft perform various maneuvers to test the airworthiness of the aircraft. Most of the different flight profiles he requested were improvised by the flight crew on the spot. An altitude of 40,000 feet was maintained for some of the flight (where the two AOA sensors froze).

In VFR weather conditions, the aircraft was at 3,000 feet when they attempted a low speed handling check; <u>Certified Test Pilots perform this maneuver at 14,000 feet</u>. The pilot slowed the airspeed to 99 knots, the aircraft was in landing configuration (landing gear were down, flaps extended).

Airbus' fly-by-wire system chose the two AOA sensors that agreed, which were frozen in one position, the auto-trim system then moved the

---

[104] The Aviation Herald, "Crash: Air New Zeeland A320 near Perpignan on Nov 27th 2008, impacted Mediterranean Sea", Simon Hradecky, 9/16/2010

horizontal stabilizer to maximum, giving the airplane a 19° pitch up angle, and the A320 subsequently stalled.

The crew did not call out the aircraft speed, which should have been done during that low speed handling check. They lost situational awareness. The aircraft was pitch up, slowing down, when they realized the aircraft was in a critical condition, going as slow as 40 knots. Although they applied full throttle to try and save the aircraft, it had slowed down too much to allow them to recover at such a low altitude from an airplane stall.

Knowing how the Airbus A320 crashed, is there anything about it that can relate to an aircraft carrying revenue passengers on a scheduled flight, like JT610 or ET302? The obvious answer is NO!

REDUNDANCY

As I understand the current MCAS implementation, only one FCC is active at a time; MCAS software resides in each FCC. After each flight the 737 MAX choses a different FCC to use on the next flight.

Installed in the 737 MAX are two FCC's.

My knowledge of the FCC only applies to former versions, not the current one installed in the 737 MAX. Earlier versions of the FCC had two CPU's inside them. The two CPU's ran almost identical code, side by side, and each CPU had associated hardware which was considered one channel.

A third CPU would monitor the other two CPU's health, and if one failed it automatically switched to the channel that was working. (It would run similar software as the other two CPU's did, and thereby activating the channel that agreed with it.)

When in the cockpit a pilot chooses the Captain's side, then most of the boxes in the avionics bay labeled #1 were active and presented their information to be used by the autopilot and navigation of the 737 MAX.

Choosing the First Officer side, by selecting an arrow on the eyebrow panel in the cockpit, all of the boxes labeled #2 in the avionics bay become the active systems used by the pilots.

All flight critical avionics boxes are duplicated in commercial airplanes.

If not already part of the MCAS software, a slight change could be made to the MCAS software to be active on whichever side is selected in the cockpit. Pilots need to have training that selecting either Captain or First Officer position will also result in a different FCC and its associated MCAS software to be active. (As long there is a **MCAS FAIL** indication when a failure occurs, alerting pilots to switch to the other FCC.)

By doing such a simple thing, the 737 MAX will have redundancy of MCAS.

FULL MOTION FLIGHT SIMULATOR TRAINING

Boeing needs to restore faith in the 737 MAX, and they need to win over the 737 pilot community.

Regulating bodies, such as the F.A.A. and EASA have final say over what a country's pilots need to do about being trained on a new airplane, (there are many other countries with separate Regulating Agencies as well).

In the real world, when the F.A.A. previously set a standard for training on a new aircraft manufactured in the U.S., the rest of the world follow along in lockstep.

Manufacturers on new airplanes either receive a Derivative Type Certificate, where little training is needed, or they receive a completely new Type Certificate, and then pilots need to be trained on everything, not just changes from a previous version.

Yet, in practical terms, Boeing does influence the F.A.A.'s decision. They fund permanent lobbyists on Capitol Hill in Washington D.C.; one year they spent $22 million dollars persuading Congress to back legislation they wanted. (In 2018 Boeing had 98 paid lobbyists to coerce Congress to acquiesce to their "requests"; annually they average $20 million a year on lobbying.[105])

If Boeing was to ask the F.A.A. to mandate full flight simulator training on the 737 MAX, my previous experience being an F.A.A. employee, and having a lobbyist work to fulfill my union's desires, the fix would be in, and it would happen. The opposite is also true, as is evident in the current situation surrounding the 737 MAX.

In simulator training they need to duplicate one of the scenarios that led to the crashes. Having been an instructor, and using a flight simulator in my courses, more than that needs to be done. A few similar cockpit labs need to be run, like when runaway stabilizer occurs on climb-out, or if an FCC fails 2 minutes after take-off, etc. Make flight crews use creativity to figure out what can be malfunctioning, and how to combat it. (Looking at both flights JT610 and ET302, MCAS functioned exactly as it was designed for, MCAS took control – flying both airplanes into the Earth, on purpose; it did not have a failure.)

INVESTIGATE MCAS SOFTWARE DEVELOPMENT

---

[105] The Seattle Times, "Boeing's Washington, D.C., influence network tested in 737 MAX crises", John McCormick and Bill Allison, 3/22/2019

Besides convincing pilots into being advocates for the 737 MAX ungrounding, regulators from other countries need to be brought on-board as well.

One way to do this is a full investigation of the software development of MCAS. The latest version is supposed to be 12.1, but the inquiry needs to go all the way back to the original version of MCAS software installed on the 737 MAX.

Either RTCA DO-178C or SAE ARP4754A documents should have been used to create the MCAS software. There are other options I have not discussed; Boeing could have developed its own internal software coding standard or Collins Aerospace used a military standard. (Both options would still have to be as restrictive as the other two standards I cite for civilian aircraft.)

Whatever process was used, every single step performed will have written traceability.

Each **validation test** will have recorded results: what worked and what didn't because of errors developing due to written software requirements were inadequate.

Outcomes from all **verification tests** will be documented as well: listing all of times there was a software error occurring because of the software code being written wrong.

A Business Analyst is an individual who understands what a company (Boeing) is trying to accomplish in software for their end users (pilots). These people then monitor the company (Collins Aerospace) who actually codes the software, looking at verification and validation testing. It is a constant process achieved though diligence to produce a final product that does what was intended. However, the person Boeing employed in this role (or team of people) failed miserably when the **AOA DISAGREE** warning is considered. Boeing wanted it in all 737 MAX airplanes, but that did not happen.

It goes on and on. No software development is conducted without everything being transcribed so anyone making changes 10 years later will be able to see the raw code and the thoughts behind why it was written that way.

If this is done, and just the final results of the inquiry were made public, then I think other countries will validate that the 737 MAX is safe to fly in. (Other country's Regulatory Agencies may want to see all of the actual results, but they should sign an agreement not to publish them, keeping Boeing's trade secrets private.)

SLIDING SCALE

At first, back in 2012, Boeing's chief pilot on a stationary simulator felt a problem on the yoke when conducting a Windup Turn, at high speed and cruise altitude. Engineers invented MCAS to solve this problem and gave MCAS software the authority to move the horizontal stabilizer 0.6 units of movement.

In 2016, a new chief pilot for Boeing felt a problem with the yoke at low altitudes and low speeds, then mentioned this to the design team of the 737 MAX. MCAS software was subsequently changed and the Boeing's software engineers gave it authority to move the horizontal stabilizer 2.5 units at all speeds.

Since I'm not privy to how the software code is written, MCAS should have its authority be a function of speed and altitude; a sliding scale. At slower speeds and low altitudes MCAS needs to respond with bigger movements at slow speeds, and less movement at higher speeds to achieve longitudinal stability.

By doing this the end result will be achieved, MCAS will no longer drive the 737 into the ground at low altitudes and high speed.

Pilots and Regulatory Agencies I think will approve of this change I recommend.

OTHER IDEAS TO MAKE THE 737 MAX SAFE

Any new Airworthiness Directive (AD) about MCAS, should have maintenance instructions to check the angle of both AOA sensors. Doing so would ensure flight safety, also creating a public perception the aircraft is safe, because every aircraft is starting from a good baseline. (I personally know of a few AD's that required some physical maintenance action.)

Why doesn't MCAS software poll both AOA sensors **BEFORE** V1 speed is achieved. Once a 737 MAX is moving down the runway at 80 knots, both AOA sensors will be active and accurate. If the two AOA sensors disagree, have the pilots abort the landing. Simple. Display a **MCAS FAIL** message in red, and train pilots to be aware of observing their PFD's for this error message before reaching V1 speed on the runway.

Each 737 MAX has 2 Radio Altimeters (RALT's), which provide a usable signal whenever the airplane is above 2,000 feet above ground level. I know these signals are already fed to both FCC's because they are what should prevent an **AOA DISAGREE** warning below 400 feet of altitude. MCAS software can use these signals from preventing a 2.5° nose down when it is at high speed and low altitude (below 2,000 feet). Just another failsafe to be designed into the MCAS software.

Have Boeing's rocket scientists create an imaginary pocket around the aircraft, like TCAS II (Traffic Collision Avoidance System) does, allowing MCAS to function safely, as advertised only in areas where it was intended for. Make the pocket disappear on takeoff, and make it small or large, depending on air conditions, airframe configuration, and speed. If software could be written by scientists, taking in all scenarios,

MCAS would be a great addition to aircraft safety – and the airframe and engines do not have to be altered in any way.

LOTTERY

Organize a lottery. No, I have not lost my mind.

My older brother has drummed into my daughter and I that we are never to present management with a problem without giving at least one possible solution.

Some of my thoughts on what I think are required to gain 737 MAX pilots and Regulatory Agencies support were elaborated in the above paragraphs.

But how do you win back customers flying for business or vacation, wanting them to get back into the 737 MAX?

I propose a lottery for free tickets on the 737 MAX, devised by each airline's marketing department. Coordinate with IATA so no airline promotional program will collide with another one's idea.

Target an audience that needs to be won back, to get the rest of the general public flying on the 737 MAX again. Market and advertise it, get Boeing to underwrite it (they will sell more airplanes again), **and once the aircraft has been changed to be safe**, everyone is a winner in the long run.

19. WHAT DID BOEING KNOW AND WHEN DID THEY KNOW?

Some pilots think the AOA sensor display is unnecessary; in a truly fly-by-wire aircraft those pilots would be correct, however, the 737 MAX is not fly-by-wire. For decades the NTSB has been recommending that the AOA information be displayed in the cockpit as an indicator. Boeing knows this, but since the NTSB can only "recommend", this advice was ignored on the 737 MAX.

During the summer of 2017, Boeing engineers had discovered that the **AOA DISAGREE** warning did not function in over 80% of the aircraft delivered.

November 27, 2018, at an Allied Pilots Association (American Airlines union) meeting was held with Boeing officials at their Fort Worth, TX, headquarters. One person in that meeting recorded audio. After this meeting the President of the union filed a Freedom of Information request for documents relating to the 737 MAX (he was unsatisfied with Boeing's statements).

Attending that meeting from Boeing were:[106]
- Mike Sinnett, Vice-President of Product & Safety
- Craig Bomben, a senior test pilot for Boeing
- John Moloney, Director of Transportation Policy (he's a senior lobbyist at Boeing)
- Alan Smolinski, Sales Director for the Americas

Pilots for American Airlines argued for an FAA emergency Airworthiness Directive, effectively grounding the 737 MAX fleet until the MCAS software was fixed. Boeing managers denied their request.

---

[106] Wall Street Journal, "Between Two Deadly Crashes, Boeing Moved Haltingly to Make 737 MAX Fixes", Andy Pasztor, Andrew Tangel and Alison Sider, 4/1/2019

During that meeting many things came up that surprised even me.

Mike Sinnett stated that it was not clear that the plane (737 MAX 8) caused the crash. Although he did not verbally say it, he implied that the foreign flight crew caused the crash due to pilot error. (Later, on 5/15/2019, in a U.S. House hearing, Congressman Sam Graves did not imply, he accused those dead pilots of making multiple errors in the cockpit causing the crash).[107]

(One flight crew during their normal full flight simulator training tried to duplicate the conditions of flight ET302 at a higher altitude; they were U.S. pilots, knew about MCAS, and were only able to avoid a crash by using the "roller-coaster maneuver" – but in doing so lost 8,000 ft. of altitude – flight ET302 never obtained an altitude of 8,000 ft[108])

Mr. Sinnett also stated Boeing did not want to overwhelm pilots with unnecessary information (about MCAS).[109] No reference to MCAS software was in the 737 MAX training, neither was in the Aircraft Flight Manual, because Boeing "did not want to give the pilots too much information".

He went on to say that a pilot might fly a 737 MAX a million miles and maybe once, if ever, run into a situation that MCAS would be a factor in. (One million miles at cruising speed of the 737 MAX translates out to less than 2,000 flight hours.)

Hard to imagine, but he kept talking and digging Boeing into a deeper hole. Another thing he said was the 737 MAX had its design

---

[107] Washington Post, "FAA chief pilot says pilot decisions contributed to Boeing 737 Max crashes", Michael Laris, Lori Aratani and Ashley Halsey III, 5/15/2019
[108] The Seattle Times, "How much was pilot error a factor in the Boeing 737 MAX crashes?", Dominic Gates, 5/15/2019
[109] Business Insider, ""Boeing dismissed fears of a 2nd 737 Max crash when confronted by pilots after the plane's first disaster, leaked audio reportedly reveals", Sinead Baker, 5/15/2019

criteria so that MCAS software and the pilot were to work in tandem. Boeing relied on pilots previous training to control the pitch axis of the aircraft. (Yet, no pilot was trained on MCAS software that essentially created a fly-by-wire 737 for pitch, or how Boeing disabled the safeguards that pilots had relied on in the past for pitch trim control.)

Another thing he said was that MCAS was part of mission critical software, and Boeing did not want to rush and change it.

Mr. Sinnett told the assembled pilots that Boeing was working on a software patch for MCAS, and it should be delivered within the next 6 weeks. (Of course, he was wrong, as of July 2019 it has been 9 months and it still isn't finished).

Boeing's management team at that meeting stated the AOA DISAGREE warning worked on the ground.[110] (They either blatantly lied, or worse, were ignorant of how the MCAS software functioned.)

So much is wrong with what they told the American Airline's 737 pilots, it's hard to unpack.

First, the AOA DISAGREE warning is only allowed to be displayed on the PFD after the airplane climbs above 400 feet (RALT input is supposed to prevent it). If it was active on the ground, as an aircraft began its taxi to the runway it's warning would go off many times. The AOA sensors are mechanical, look like small weathervanes, and they bounce as the airplane goes over any bumps on the taxiway at a slow ground speed.

Next, 13 months previous to this meeting, Boeing knew only 20% of the 737 MAX fleet had this warning activated. A customer had to purchase the "Error Notification Kit" from Boeing for this warning to work. They implied it worked on the entire 737 MAX fleet, satisfying

---

[110] New York Times, Boeing Believed a 737 Max Warning Light Was Standard. It Wasn't", David Gelles and Natalie Kitroeff, 5/5/2019

the American Airlines pilots. (In my opinion, they were actively trying to deceive those pilots by not being honest and telling the whole truth.)

They told those pilots this **AOA DISAGREE** warning wasn't even needed; it was not a safety of flight warning.

After the second 737 MAX crash (ET302) Boeing has erroneously blamed the delay of the software patch on the U.S. government shut-down. (All safety related functions in the government were staffed during the shut-down, so there was no 35-day delay.)

Again, before the end of November, Mike Sinnett met with the Air Line Pilots Association (ALPA) at their headquarters near Washington, D.C. ALPA is a professional pilot union representing 62,000 commercial pilots, and he repeated most of his previous statements (there was no audio recording of this meeting that I'm aware of).

Another aspect of what was known before the fatal accidents of the 737 MAX involves Boeing's Board of Directors.

Not everyone has sat in on a Board of Directors meeting; one of my various duties I had in the PASS Union was to sit in on their Board Meetings, being a nationally elected union officer. So, I do have a little experience on how Board meetings are conducted and who's typically involved.

In business, being selected to be on the Board of Directors is very prestigious, and very lucrative. Boeing pays a stipend to their board members of $324,000 per year, for attending 6 meetings a year.[111]

Duties for Boeing's Board members are simple: hire or fire the company CEO, set the pay of Boeing senior executives, and question top executive decisions – are they made in the long-term interests of the company?

---

[111] Washington Post, " 'Safety was just a given': Inside Boeing's boardroom amid the 737 MAX crisis ", Douglas MacMillan, 5/5/2019

That last task is where the Boeing Board of Directors looked at short term financial interests, not considering the long-term consequences of what Boeing management was doing to produce the 737 MAX, impacting its future by placing such large fuel-efficient engines changing its aerodynamics adversely.

Since they hired Dennis Muilenburg as CEO, share prices were up almost 400%, the factory was turning out twice the output of airplanes with a workforce that had been reduced by 7%; the Board recently set his pay at $23.4 million a year in 2019.

Every face on the Board of Directors is famous or already rich. Caroline Kennedy joined in 2017, and the latest to take their place on this Board is Nikki Haley, she was the former U.S. Ambassador to the U.N.

Not one of them, except Dennis Muilenburg (who was both CEO and Chairman of the Board), had the needed experience to question long-term ramifications about the 737 MAX decisions. Most surprisingly for a company who preaches they believe in safety first, not one Board member has a background in aircraft safety, and there is no mention of safety in their charter.

Sometime around the Paris Airshow of 2011, when Airbus took over 600 orders on the A320NEO, Boeing's Board had to have discussed whether it was better to create a new airplane design or just repurpose the old 737 airplane to be a fuel-efficient aircraft.

Only the CEO, who had increased Boeing's share price (which benefitted him), had the experience to debate the safety trade-offs needed to reuse the ancient 737 design. They voted for the tired old 737 design be used to create the 737 MAX, not getting into the details of exchanging aircraft safety for company profits.

Comparing the clean sheet design of the 787 that had run over budget by billions of U.S. dollars and delivered 3 years late, to a clean sheet design for a new aircraft was unacceptable to the Board. People on the Board voted with Dennis Muilenburg – the new aircraft would be based on the technically ancient 737 design, saving time and money. Safety issues about re-using a 50-year-old design were not discussed.[112]

---

[112] Washington Post, " 'Safety was just a given': Inside Boeing's boardroom amid the 737 MAX crisis ", Douglas MacMillan, 5/5/2019

20. MEETINGS / INVESTIGATIONS

Boeing began deliveries of the 737 MAX back on 5/6/2017.

Boeing's first committee knew that 80% of the delivered 737 MAX airplanes did not have the **AOA DISAGREE** warning. They also understood that any future 737 MAX manufactured airplanes would have the AOA warning only if the "safety package" was to be installed (20%).

> QUESTION: WHY DIDN'T BOEING CHANGE THE MCAS SOFTWARE, AFTER FINDING IT HAD AN ERROR, FOR THE NEWLY MANUFACTURED 737 MAX AIRPLANES?

After discussing the software error back in 2017, this first committee agreed it could be fixed in the ***next*** software patch. Their conclusion was delivered to Boeing management 13 months BEFORE the first crash, JT610. A software patch to MCAS did occur on January 25, 2019, it did not include this fix (it did include a "fix" to handle flap switch failure). Both flights, JT610 and ET302, were on airplanes manufactured in 2018. Maybe if Boeing had made a change in software earlier, those flights wouldn't have crashed.

After the JT610 crash in 2018, Boeing convened an internal Safety Review Board (SRB),[113] to look at the same software error that did not display an **AOA DISAGREE** warning on the pilot's PFD. These engineers and managers came to their conclusions in early November 2018. Although they considered this software error to be "low risk", and "not adversely affecting safety", Boeing did eventually inform the F.A.A. in November 2018 about a software "problem".

---

[113] CNN, "Boeing knew about problems with the 737 Max the year before Lion Air crash and did nothing about them", Patricia DiCarlo, 5/5/2019

Once they were informed, the F.A.A. also assembled a committee of mid-level managers to study the problem.[114]

The F.A.A. mid-level managers debated this software problem until February 2019. Eventually they arrived at a determination, this was not a serious enough issue to ground the fleet. Of course, just days later was the second 737 MAX crash, ET302. (Just to avoid confusion, this is a separate group composed of only F.A.A. mid-level managers. Another group of F.A.A. Inspectors conferred about this exact same issue, but they only had responsibility for Southwest Airlines fleet.)

Not only did these managers make the wrong call, they never informed senior F.A.A. managers about the MCAS software problem Boeing discovered which was involved in the first crash of an aircraft. (Criminal Negligence?) Neither did they inform other F.A.A. certificate management offices about the problem that could affect American Airlines or United, all flying the 737 MAX. (United Airlines was informed of this software problem 4 months after Southwest Airlines found out about it.[115])

The F.A.A. is sponsoring a task force made up of international regulatory agencies, to review the issue of MCAS, and its fix, called the "Joint Authorities Technical Review" (JATR).[116] Former head of the U.S. National Transportation Safety Board (NTSB), Christopher Hart, is leading the task force, co-chaired by NASA.

Representatives from 9 different country regulating agencies attended (Australia, Brazil, Canada, China, EASA, Indonesia, Japan,

---

[114] Wall Street Journal, "Boeing Knew About Safety-Alert Problem for a Year Before Telling FAA, Airlines", Andy Pasztor, Andrew Tangel and Alison Sider, 5/5/2019

[115] Wall Street Journal, "Boeing Knew About Safety-Alert Problem for a Year Before Telling FAA, Airlines", Andy Pasztor, Andrew Tangel and Alison Sider, 5/5/2019

[116] Wall Street Journal, "Boeing Looks to Build Overseas Support for MAX Fix", Andy Pasztor, Andrew Tangel and Robert Wall, 4/10/2019

Singapore, and United Arab Emirates), and representatives from the FAA and NASA were present as well. Their first meetings occurred on the last week of April 2019. All involved have agreed to a 90-day time frame, before they issue a final report.[117] Preliminary conclusions are expected much sooner.

Regardless of the JATR findings, the F.A.A. has stated their decision to unground the 737 MAX will be separate from any results from that review.[118]

The F.A.A. did empower another panel of experts concerning the 737 MAX airplanes, it's called the Technical Advisory Board (TAB); members include the U.S. Air Force, NASA, and the Department of Transportation. This Board is to examine the MCAS software "fix" and is specifically tasked with identifying issues were further investigation is needed. After the group finishes, they will make recommendations to the F.A.A. about MCAS software. All of this is to occur before the F.A.A. ungrounds the 737 MAX.[119]

On May 23, 2019, the International Air Transport Association (IATA) held a meeting in Montreal, Canada, its headquarters. Initially they intended to invite 28 members who currently fly or have ordered the 737 MAX. After the first public announcement for this meeting they opened it up so any of the 290 airlines they represent could attend. Approximately 80% of world-wide passenger traffic is represented by this association. It was a precursor to their annual meeting held in Seoul, South Korea; where about 200 airline CEO's attended.[120]

---

[117] Airways, "BOEING 737 MAX: FAA to Meet with Multi-Nation Certification Board", Leila Chaibi, James Field and Jamie Clarke, 4/22/2019

[118] Reuters, "U.S. FAA, global aviation regulators to meet May 23 on Boeing 737 MAX, David Shepardson, 4/25/2019

[119] Business Insider, "The FAA is so concerned about the future of Boeing's 737 MAX that it is bringing in NASA and the Air Force to help ensure it is safe to fly again", Sinead Baker, 5/8/2019

[120] Reuters, "Trade gloom, rising oil, Boeing 737 MAX woes to cloud aviation summit", Heekyong Yang and Tracy Rucinski, 5/30/2019

IATA was founded after WWII and has evolved into a lobbying group and clearing house for information regarding world-wide aviation.

Focusing on having all countries recognize each other's regulatory authority in aviation, the IATA is trying to get the world to unground the 737 MAX at the same time.

Logic behind this May 23rd meeting was to get all regulators on the same page. IATA is trying to prevent a future where each country's regulatory body grants a separate certificate for the same aircraft. In the case of Boeing's 737 MAX, more than 40 simultaneous certifications would be required if each nation conducted individual certifications, all ending on different dates.

Also, on May 23, 2019, the International Civil Aviation Organization (ICAO) met with 2 officials from the F.A.A. in Montreal Canada and received a briefing on the state of the 737 MAX airplanes. ICAO is a unique entity, they are responsible for the world aviation community (about 196 countries), able to make recommendations like NTSB, coordinate future advancements in aviation like EASA does for Europe, and securing Airworthiness Safety Inspectors for countries that cannot afford a separate regulating body. I am just giving broad brush strokes, ICAO does even more than the things I identify here.

Updates from the F.A.A. and Boeing on the 737 MAX were the topic of discussion with ICAO.

Again, on May 23, 2019 the F.A.A. sponsored a meeting in Fort Worth, Texas. International regulatory agencies were invited; they tried to convince attendees that no country needs to perform their own individual System Safety Analysis of the MCAS software.

Countries that accepted that invitation were: Brazil, Canada, China, Ethiopia, various European countries, and Indonesia; Boeing was excluded; over 33 countries were represented at that meeting.

In F.A.A. speak, that was a dog & pony show. The F.A.A. has let it be known that they will wait for no other country to agree on the correct solution to the MCAS software, they plan on being the first country to unground the 737 MAX. Just like they were almost the last country to ground that airplane (determined by U.S. politics, not fact driven from data on each FDR).

Looking at the list of safety experts picked by the Secretary of the D.O.T., Elaine Chao, to the [121]Safety Oversight and Certification Advisory Committee (SOCAC) on the 737 MAX, it's a D.O.T Special Committee but created by the F.A.A. Reauthorization Act of 2018. Not one is an expert in aircraft certification, software System Safety Analysis, DER's or AR's. The blue-ribbon panel of experts consist of:
- (Co-Chair) – Darren McDew, a former General of the U.S. Transport command
- (Co-Chair) – Lee Moak; former President of Air Lines Pilot Association
- Amy Pritchett; former NASA Aviation Safety Program Director
- Gretchen Haskins; CEO of HeliOffshoe LTD (former U.S. officer)
- Kenneth Hylander; Chief Safety Officer at Amtrak (former airline pilot)
- J. David Grizzle; Chairman of the Board, Republic Airways (former F.A.A. General Counsel)

Realistically, how are they going to answer specific safety questions about certifying the 737 MAX? All of the current (July 2019) members of the SOCAC are just political picks. Credentials and titles, but no real hands-on experience in aircraft certification or airworthiness oversight.

---

[121] Reuters, "U.S. names experts to Boeing certification review panel", David Shepardson, 4/22/2019

SOCAC has no specific deadline but are expected to deliver something in writing before 2020. This committee has a charter enabling them to exist until May 2025.

In the solicitation for members to voluntarily join the SOCAC, it was supposed to consist of;
1. General Aviation Manufacturing
2. Commercial Aviation Manufacturing
3. Avionics Manufacturing
4. Aviation Labor (union representation)
5. F.A.A. Inspectors & Engineers
6. General Aviation Operators
7. Air Carrier Operators (airlines)
8. UAV – Manufacturing & Operators
9. Experts in Aviation Safety
10. Aviation Maintenance
11. Airport Owners and Operators[122]

The named individuals to SOCAC does not seem to represent all of the above categories.

One thing the F.A.A. has NOT investigated is the NASA database, Aviation Safety Reporting System (ASRS). Before the 737 MAX 8 crash on March 10, 2019, five American pilots reported problems with the 737 MAX nose being forced down automatically during take-off. NASA just accumulates data; it does not issue reports. Boeing has claimed none of those 5 ASRS reports about the 737 MAX going automatically nose-down involve MCAS, because pilots had engaged the autopilot. Yet, on the second crash (ET302), the autopilot was engaged, but kicked off because of the AOA sensor. (I think that MCAS software has more than one problem.)

One day after the 2nd crash, on March 11, 2019, four different whistleblowers called a hotline to give damning information about the manufacture of the Boeing 737 MAX.

---

[122] D.O.T., Solicitation of Nominations for Appointment to the Safety Oversight and Certification Advisory Committee, 3/25/2019

Department of Justice, Fraud Section, in Washington D.C., have convened a Grand Jury to criminally investigate the 737 MAX 8 manufacturing processes and decisions made. (Basically, I think they are investigating whether Boeing has covered up any damning information.) Subpoenas have been issued; the FBI has conducted interviews. Anyone outside of aviation may just accept this as the new normal. **IT IS NOT!**

National Transportation Safety Board (NTSB) investigates crashes. When someone famous dies in an aircraft crash, NTSB investigates. When 3 or more people die, the NTSB investigates (2 or less deaths, the F.A.A. is normally delegated by the NTSB to conduct the field investigation).

I have been reading NTSB crash reports for more than 30 years, I cannot remember one that had a simultaneous criminal investigation. **AFTER** the final NTSB crash report, a few times there may have been criminal investigations because of something unearthed by the NTSB, but none come to my mind.

Please be reminded that an investigation may not lead to criminal charges, just like the results of the final Muellar Report did not indict the U.S. President. (Other people were not only charged, but convicted, during the investigation by the legal team headed by Robert Muellar.)

D.O.T. Inspector General Report, 6/29/2011[123]

Basically, this report was the first time the F.A.A. ODA program was looked at, after being fully implemented in 2009.

Significant Findings:

---

[123] D.O.T., I.G. Report #AV-2011-136, Oversight – Organization Designation Authority (ODA)

1. FAA engineers with oversight were not enforcing compliance with regulations
2. No tracking of ODA team members had been done by the F.A.A.
3. More than 80 manufacturers had an ODA
5. F.A.A. is losing direct supervisory connection with ODA team members

G.A.O. Testimony to Congress, 2015 [124]

F.A.A. does not have sufficient resources to provide oversight on the ODA's that have already been granted.

D.O.T. Inspector General Report, 2015[125]

(Even the D.O.T. Inspector General used contractors in preparing this report – evidence of systemic staffing problems government wide… IG investigators outsourcing vital functions)

This second audit was not only on ODA oversight, but also looked at F.A.A. staffing for certification offices during 2014.

Significant Findings:
1. F.A.A. management was not staffing certification offices effectively
2. The vendor supplying Boeing fuselages was not inspected at all by F.A.A. certification personnel
3. A total of 44% of the F.A.A. oversight personnel of ODA's did not complete a single inspection item for that whole year (everyone with ODA responsibility must complete one inspection item each year, per F.A.A. Order 8100.15B)

[124] GAO Testimony before Senate Sub-Committee on Aviation, "Aviation Certification", 4/21/2015

[125] D.O.T. I.G. Audit Report #AV-2016-001, "FAA Lacks an Effective Staffing Model and Risk-Based Oversight Process for Organization Designation Authorization", 10/15/2015

4. Another F.A.A. Inspector who had oversight of 400 individual ODA team members, only reviewed the work of 9 of them
5. Of 310 ODA employees located at many different vendor locations, the F.A.A. only performed oversight of 4% of those inside the U.S. Overseas there were 101 ODA employees at foreign vendor locations, and the F.A.A. performed oversight on none of them
6. F.A.A. certification personnel had training "gaps" (i.e. they were not fully trained) but doing the work (not even being "mentored" by a F.A.A. employee who had training)

D.O.T. Inspector General Statement, 3/27/2019

In this statement to Congress the Inspector General (IG) gave a perspective over the entire Air Transportation System.

Significant Findings:
1. In 14 CFR 121.424 the IG pointed out that there were changes made by the F.A.A., effective 3/12/2019, it concerned pilot training. Mandated was the ability for pilots to recover from upset conditions, specifically stall training, flying the aircraft manually.
2. Coincidently, the IG also found that no airline possessed a 737 MAX simulator that could replicate stall conditions in the 737 MAX.

Until the end of 2019 no U.S. airline will have a 737 MAX flight simulator, currently Boeing has one, Canada has one, as does Ethiopian Air – none of which can duplicate MCAS as of June 2019.

THINK ABOUT IT:

Has any U.S. airline complied with the newly implemented regulations?

21. ODDS & ENDS

Passenger accommodation in the 737 MAX can range from 138 to 230, based on how the customer (airline) wants it configured.

There are more flavors than just the 737 MAX 8 and 737 MAX 9; in development is the 737 MAX 7 and 737 MAX 10.

Back in 2017, Boeing had gross sales of $93.4 billion, made a net profit of $9.6 billion, and paid $13.3 million in federal taxes (i.e., nothing). For 2018, Boeing had gross sales of $101 billion.

List price for a 737 MAX 8 is $121.6 million.[126] When an airline purchases many of these airframes at a time, they get a significant cost break; they pay 40% when it is manufactured, and 60% when it's delivered.

On March 13, 2019, the F.A.A. grounded all 737 MAX 8, and all the other countries in the world followed suit, except for those 50 countries who had already grounded them on March 11, 2019. Realistically, the F.A.A. was one of the last ones to ban the 737 MAX from flight. (To be technically correct, President Trump ordered the F.A.A. to ground the 737 MAX fleet;[127] there was no data driven decision as the acting F.A.A. Administrator, Daniel Elwell, wants the public to believe. Grounding the 737 MAX in the U.S. was a purely political decision.)

At the factory, by the end of June 2019, they will have about 225 of the 737 MAX aircraft parked.[128] If they are grounded until Christmas

---

[126] 24/7 WALL ST, "How Much Does a Boeing 737 MAX Cost?", Paul Ausick, 3/11/2019

[127] Washington Post, " 'Safety was just a given': Inside Boeing's boardroom amid the 737 MAX crisis ", Douglas MacMillan, 5/5/2019

[128] Bloomberg, "Boeing Max Grounding Endangers Cash Machine Adored by Wall Street", Julie Johnsson, 4/23/2019

2019, there could be as many as 500 737 MAX airplanes parked around the factory.

Once a fuselage is delivered to the factory it takes just 9 days to roll out of the factory as a completed 737 MAX.

Even though Boeing slowed down its factory from producing 57 per month of the 737 MAX aircraft, down to 42 per month[129] in April 2019, it will be parking about $4 BILLION of 737 MAX airplanes every month thereafter.

Boeing began parking 737 MAX airplanes in their employees parking lot in June 2019. After reading 14 CFR 21.197, I wonder how the F.A.A. can justify Boeing flying those airplanes to another location using a ferry flight permit? (2 identical airplanes as those being manufactured crashed on take-off, and the F.A.A. is letting Boeing fly 40 a month of those 737 MAX airplanes soar to other locations?) In a just world, they would be forced to quit manufacturing those unsafe aircraft, once they run out of parking places at their factory.

Worldwide delivery of the 737 MAX 8 aircraft in March 2019 stood at 387. The U.S. had 72 of them (Southwest Airlines = 34; American Airlines = 24; United Airlines = 14). Over 300 of the 737 MAX aircraft had been delivered to foreign airlines. (Boeing is America's largest exporter at 0.2% of U.S. GDP, whereas all agriculture exports in the U.S. only amounts to 1.0% of GDP.)

It was forecast that Boeing would deliver 600 aircraft in 2019, with the 737 MAX 8 accounting for 90% of them; they have booked orders for 4,600 more 737 MAX aircraft.

Right now (August 2019), Boeing has slated $4.9 billion dollars to reimburse airlines for all of the lost revenue to them, because they had to park perfectly good airplanes that Boeing had sold them. Of course,

---

[129] Reuters, "Boeing sees FAA approving software fix in May, MAX ungrounding in July: sources", Tracy Rucinski and Eric M. Johnson, 4/23/2019

they are flawed, but Boeing won't admit to selling flawed aircraft. (Admit Nothing)

In the U.S. alone, those 72 aircraft (737 MAX 8), represent 350,000 seats not being filled each week. Southwest Airlines has to cancel 150 flights each day its planes are parked. American Airlines has to cancel 115 flights a day for each day its planes are parked.[130] United is going to start averaging 60 cancelations a day by August 2019.[131] As the grounding of the 737 MAX drags on, airlines that had planned on adding even more of those airplanes to their fleet have to cancel future flights; so air travel will definitely be impacted for the Christmas travel season in 2019.

One analyst has concluded that 40,000,000 seats have not been filled world-wide, because of the grounded 737 MAX, and all of the deliveries that have not happened.

Analysts predict losses of $75,000 per airframe, per day, for each airframe parked; that figures out to be $30 million a day for the entire fleet of parked 737 MAX aircraft. There is also the added cost all airlines incur because they are not filling passenger seats on the 737 Max airplanes that should have been delivered. (As of June 2019, airlines are absorbing the costs of grounding their 737 MAX fleet, and that does not include the associated costs of 737 MAX airplanes not being delivered to them on schedule.)

Costs for grounding the 737 MAX fleet keep mounting every day, some of which are:
- $2,000 a day parking fees[132] for each one, and more for daily maintenance on them

---

[130] Wall Street Journal, "Boeing Woes Spread at Two Airlines", Alison Sider, Andy Pasztor and Doug Cameron, 4/15/2019

[131] Market Watch, "United and Southwest are still cancelling thousands of flights because of the Boeing 737 Max grounding", Jacob Passey, 6/28/2019

[132] Bloomberg, "Boeing's 737 Max Bills Include $2,00 a Month to Park Each Grounded Jet", Julie Johnsson and Mary Schlangenstein, 5/24/2019

- It takes about 80 man-hours per plane to put a 737 MAX into storage
  Another 150 man-hours are needed to remove a 737 MAX from storage[133]

Boeing must reimburse airlines for:
- Each cancelled flight
- Every replacement airplane lease cost, used to replace a 737 MAX
- Increased fuel cost on replacement airplanes
- All revenue lost, because of delayed deliveries
- Pilots are suing Boeing for lost wages
- Investors are suing Boeing for not disclosing 737 MAX problems ($45 billion lost)
- Replacement aircraft for the 737 MAX costs a minimum of $300,000 a month[134]

China is pursuing Boeing for 3 months of having 96 aircraft parked, for an estimated $580 million.[135] Southwest Airlines says it has lost $200 million because of the 737 MAX grounding for 3 months. Imagine if the 737 MAX isn't flying again until Christmas of 2020, the grounding costs to Boeing become staggering.

To add insult to injury, Airbus has stepped up its production of the A320NEO to 60 per month, while Boeing has backed down its production to 42 per month[136]. Keep in mind Boeing cannot sell any 737 MAX produced, until the F.A.A. and other countries agree there is a MCAS software fix.

---

[133] Reuters, "Exclusive: US airlines expect Boeing 737 MAX jets need up to 150 hours of work before flying again", Tracy Rucinski, 5/23/2019

[134] Wall Street Journal, "Boeing's MAX Grounding Lifts Firms That Rent Out Airplanes", Robert Wall and Daniel Michaels

[135] Associated Press, "China to Help Airlines Seeking Compensation from Boeing 737 Max Grounding", 5/24/2019

[136] Wall Street Journal, "Boeing to Cut 737 MAX Production", Doug Cameron, 4/5/2019

In June 2019, Spirit AeroSystems, which manufactures the 737 MAX fuselage, is forcing its workforce to put in 32 hours per week, until Boeing gets the 737 MAX flying again.[137] They even offered early retirements, which 200 workers took advantage of.[138] Costs of not flying the 737 MAX are now starting to trickle down to their 900 vendors.

Ripples from the 737 MAX grounding are even spreading to the airlines. Iceland Air fired their 21 pilots who had been flying the 737 MAX, and while 24 other pilots were in training to learn to fly it, they were let go as well.[139] Iceland Air has three 737 MAX and more on order. Southwest has been quoted in news reports that they have too many pilots, now that their fleet of 737 MAX airplanes are grounded.

China has stated that they will not receive another 737 MAX until it goes through an entire re-certification process, taking about a year.

All of the above shows how much pressure is on Boeing to get the 737 MAX flying again. It's not just a matter of profitability, but their reputation is also at stake (read future orders).

Boeing appears to be tone deaf, recently announcing the replacement of 30% of their inspection workforce, to be replaced by automation;[140] they call this the "QA Transformation Plan".

If "re-assigning" 900 Quality Assurance Inspectors was not enough, Boeing now proposes to eliminate physically testing their new aircraft

---

[137] CNN, "Spirit cuts workweek in wake of 737 MAX groundings: union", Sanjana Shivdas, 6/7/2019

[138] The Wall Street Journal, "GE's New Billion-Dollar Problem? Boeing's MAX", Thomas Gryta, 8/1/2019

[139] Luxury Travel Diary (website), "You're Fired! Pilots their Jobs at Airlines Lose Faith in the B737 MAX", 6/9/2019

[140] USA Today, "Amid scrutiny over 737 Max, Boeing to replace 900 inspectors. And union is not happy", Chris Woodyard, 5/6/2019

designs and replace them with computer simulations.[141] Their goal is to do "certification by analysis" to further slash development costs. (Look how much good that did for the 737 MAX, knowing that is what they did for much of the MCAS certification.) When asked for comment, F.A.A. spokesperson, Lynn Lundsford, noted how the government relies on manufacturer's decades of experience building aircraft; so yes, it looks like the F.A.A. is on board with this idea too.

    Commercial airplanes use autopilot extensively. Pilots are 100% in manual control of the aircraft during take-off and landing, in-between the autopilot usually does the work. There are exceptions to this general rule. If an airplane is rated for Category III landing (each airline calls this by a different name), and the crew is certified for such operations, the autopilot can land the plane.

    Commercial pilots sometimes remark that they are losing touch with hand flying because less than 10% of their time is spent in manual control of the aircraft.

    Designing the 737 MAX, Boeing stuck with paper manuals for the pilots, it did not digitize its instructions and checklists, to be displayed on the glass cockpit. They did this to avoid having to make pilots go through level "D" flight simulator training. Although, if the instructions were digitized, the flight crew in JT610 would not have had to flip through paper manuals to find something that might apply, killing valuable time. Instead, a few pushes of the buttons could have revealed everything they could know.

    English is the world's language for international air traffic control.

    Of the approximately 14,000 planes in commercial service worldwide, both passenger and cargo, Boeing makes about half of them.

---

[141] Reuters, "Exclusive: Boeing seeking to reduce scope, duration of some physical tests for new aircraft sources", Eric M. Johnson, 6/16/2019

Chicago is the new home of Boeing headquarters, since it moved from Seattle, WA. Upper management appears to have lost touch with their employees who design and manufacture the aircraft for them.

A random observation. Airbus builds planes that are "fly by wire". Boeing builds airplanes that are a "kludge", part fly-by-wire, part of it is still cable driven. My definition of kludge = original design had a modification that changes it into a new configuration, that configuration has a second modification, and so on, until it becomes is a patchwork of fixes that depend upon prior fixes to work.

22. CONCLUSIONS

CRIMINALS

No longer can we let corporate criminal actions go unpunished in the U.S.

Negligent homicide is what should be the charge for every participant in Boeing's System Safety Analysis (besides the other Boeing employees I'd named earlier in this book). Each State, either Washington, or Illinois, needs to bring charges of negligent homicide to punish those who, for the motive of profit, committed conspiracy to hide relevant data that would have forced the 737 MAX airplane design to be safe.

Those who participated in Boeing's System Safety Analysis, where they assessed MCAS software as merely "hazardous" only causing a few deaths need to be held accountable. Assessing the software as "catastrophic" would have forced Boeing to incur billions of dollars in lost profits and delays, money they would have lost in share price devaluation. These criminals (in my opinion) then put their names on documents they knew were wrong, and in doing so these actions caused the loss of life to 346 individuals, so they could influence the growth of their 401(k) retirement accounts.

Please compare the above observations to the recent case of a nurse indicted for negligent homicide, for giving the wrong medication to a single patient. She looked at the first 2 letters of the medicine bottle, which were the same, and gave it to an elderly patient, who died. If that nurse is to be prosecuted for mixing up a medicine bottle, how much so for a dozen or more individuals who conspired to sell a faulty product, for personal gain?

Employees of the F.A.A. are not responsible if they make a wrong call, and people die because of it. Civil Service personnel cannot be held individually responsible for their actions (unless they committed a crime, like a accepting a bribe for such actions, or criminal negligence was involved – which I suspect is the case involving the 737 MAX). However, people the F.A.A. designate to perform those same tasks have no such protections, such as company AR's in an ODA team.

To encourage the F.A.A. to retain the responsibility for certification, a successful criminal prosecution of a Boeing AR employee would go a long way in restoring order to the oversight program. (No one in their right mind will certify a product if they can be held personally responsible if it fails, i.e., sued for financial damages.)

I personally know of 2 separate instances where F.A.A. inspectors made the wrong call, each case involved death of innocent people. Both cases were brought to court, the F.A.A. was found responsible and paid a multi-million judgement in each case. Yet, none of the inspectors involved were ever charged in court because they were indemnified by the F.A.A. (and were found not to be criminally negligent).

POOR DESIGN AND IMPLEMENTATION

Pilot error did not contribute to the crashes of either JT610 or ET302.

Neither of the flight crews on JT610 or ET302 did everything perfect. At least one U.S. flight crew reproduced the situation that a doomed flight crew faced in a 737 NG flight simulator, even knowing about MCAS, they could not escape in time to prevent a simulated crash.

Flat out – poor aircraft design must be blamed as the most significant factor in the crash, along with deficiency in documentation explaining MCAS.

The second most influential factor is how MCAS Software was designed. The way MCAS software code was executed literally drove two airplanes into the ground, exactly as a new car's autopilot can drive it into a concrete roadside pillar at high speed killing all of its occupants. Whoever approved a software change to allow 2.5° of horizontal stabilizer trim at high speeds, and that it would be reset by the pilot's Pitch Trim thumb wheels, knew nothing about flight conditions in the real world. (And if they did know, amounts to criminal negligence.)

Third, having a single point of failure using a highly unreliable AOA sensor is way up on the list of why Boeing engineered the 737 MAX to crash.

There are so many other contributing factors Boing did… removing the Pitch Trim Limit Switches from MCAS software consideration or eliminating the "yoke jerk" function to stop automatic pitch trim, are just two that must be prominently mentioned as contributing factors.

Deliberately removing any description of MCAS from all pilot manuals and differences training by Boeing has to be considered as a contributing factor in both crashes.

May I remind everyone how Boeing's CEO, Dennis Muilenburg, said in every accident it's a chain of events leading to the event. Looks to me that most of the links in the chain happened at Boeing's R&D building and its manufacturing plants that led to the crashing of two 737 Max's in 132 days.

Failure to mention the F.A.A.'s role in this 737 MAX debacle would be demeaning to all those who lost their lives.

Not only did the F.A.A. agree to Boeing's request to remove MCAS references from all pilot documentation, they even failed when they tried to correct their mistake with an emergency Airworthiness Directive. Wording in that document was vague, no detailed description of MCAS was given in the document that was supposed to correct the lack of explanation in the 737 MAX pilot manuals.

Although the F.A.A. performed less than minimum requirements required of ODA oversight at Boeing, those faults extend beyond the 737 MAX. The F.A.A. failure to do required inspections happened at many more company's ODAs, their ineptitude conducting adequate inspections is not limited to just Boeing. Deeper investigations into the F.A.A.'s oversight roles are being conducted by many government committees, and those findings will be addressed later.

MCAS DISABLED OR FAILS

Due the inherent design of the 737 MAX, it is an unstable plane to fly manually.

MCAS can never be disabled by software under any condition. Yes, it needs to be re-written on **HOW** it operates in the various modes of flight, but it should always be ON in all phases of flight.

If MCAS fails in flight, there needs to be a red warning message, like **MCAS FAIL** given to the pilots on their PFD's.

Whenever MCAS is unavailable, because it is not getting needed inputs from other systems that failed in flight, then the **MCAS FAIL** message needs to be displayed as well.

Anytime there is a **MCAS FAIL** in flight, it needs to have its own Abnormal Checklist – and because of its critical nature to correct an unstable 737 MAX, in those directions, it should tell the pilots to land at the nearest airport.

PROBLEMS TO CORRECT WITH THE F.A.A.

Funding the F.A.A. so it can again ensure air safety and no longer just promote air safety is required.

The D.O.T. Inspector General earlier findings[142] not only factually lay out the case that the F.A.A. is not just understaffing certification offices, but it has no plans to identify and correct staffing levels, let alone request additional funding for personnel who oversee aircraft manufacturers.

It is unrelated to understanding why there were 2 fatal aircraft crashes of the 737 MAX as described here, but, Unmanned Aerial Vehicles (UAV's) will be flying above our heads delivering packages and soon will morph into air taxi's in metro areas for passenger transport. (Think of taxi's that fly, from your home to anywhere in the city, without a human driver.)

If the F.A.A. is understaffed now for low-tech airplane certification, then how much more understaffed will it be when they are responsible for certifying high-tech UAV's in the future?

Boeing must be prevented from implementing their "Q.A. Transformation Plan", where they replace 900 Q.A. Inspectors with automation. Just look how many things are slipping past the quality checks already being performed on the 787 production line in newspaper reports,[143] imagine if they eliminate 1/3 of their inspection staff?

---

[142] D.O.T. I.G. Audit Report #AV-2016-001, "FAA Lacks an Effective Staffing Model and Risk-Based Oversight Process for Organization Designation Authorization", 10/15/2015

[143] The Seattle Times, "Claims of shoddy production draw scrutiny to second Boeing jet", David Gelles and Natalie Kitroeff, 4/20/2019

Someone must prevent Ali Bahrami's vision for CDO's from being implemented. He may not have had the original idea, but he is backing a plan to **eliminate all F.A.A. oversight of Boeing** (and other manufacturers) from F.A.A. Inspectors. He is personally responsible for aviation safety in the U.S., the top man at the F.A.A. for this role defending the flying public; do we have lunatics running the asylum now? I'm a retired F.A.A. official and cannot comprehend the concept of a CDO in a sane world.

OTHER OBVIOUS MATTERS

Boeing's Board of Directors need to create a position for someone who has a background in aviation safety, as it relates to manufacturing of airplanes.

QUESTION: IS BOEING TOO BIG TO FAIL?

Close to 90% of Boeing's unfilled orders are for the 737 MAX; in 2018 it accounted for 47% of commercial airplane deliveries.[144] What happens to all those vendors who supply parts to the 737 MAX if Boeing does not make it a safe airplane?

LAWSUITS

Any lawsuit against Boeing must consider penalties, to prevent such egregious behavior from ever being repeated. Boeing will consider a $500 million-dollar lawsuit as a nuisance lawsuit and gladly pay a portion of it in settlement talks (that sum would be less than 0.5% of Boeing's gross sales in 2018).

---

[144] Luxury Travel Diary (website), "Boeing in Crisis: Is this the End?", 3/24/2019

To understand Boeing's deep-pockets, they estimate their company will be forced to pay $2 billion to the airlines for just PARKING the 737 MAX for 3 months (around 387 of them world-wide were already delivered and in-service). In 2018, Boeing had over $101 billion in gross sales.

Boeing has pledged $100 million dollars to help the families of the two 737 MAX airplanes that crashed. The company targets four areas:
1. Education
2. Living expenses for families (only in hardship)
3. Community Programs
4. Economic Development

Boeing has hired Kenneth Feinberg who administered the 9/11 funds, disbursing $7.375 billion as the "Special Master", He disbursed funds that were partially based on the victims age and how much he/she would earn for the rest of their lives.

My suspicions are Boeing wants good publicity! They are just committing less than the price of a single 737 MAX 8 to buy positive public perceptions. Disbursed over 2 - 4 years and Boeing is only out the amount which would be less than what they pay out in bonus money at the end of the year to their top executives in cash and stock options.

Future orders for the 737 MAX line of aircraft stands at 5,000 in April 2019. Calculating that out, the gross revenue for that production line is over $500 billion. Boeing figures it will make a total profit of $86 billion on the 737 MAX, until it is replaced by a new design in 2030.

All lawsuits filed against Boeing; the judgement must be more than their parking fees! From my occasional brushes with civil litigation, a company will not change its fundamental behavior without a significant payout that hurts its bottom line. Such a figure should be 25% of Boeing's gross profit for one year, $25 billion.

Any lawyer suing on behalf of grieving families is going up against a "Rock-Star" team of attorneys hired by Boeing. To cover the governmental aspects and a deep background in aviation litigation is Mark Filip, who served as the former U.S. Deputy Attorney General. Next up is Richard Cullen, his law firm specializes in crisis management. Last, but not least, is William Burck, who has a practice defending white collar criminals. (again, Hmmm…) Overseeing this talented pool of legal minds is no less than J. Michael Luttig, he was a U.S. Court of Appeals judge (4th District).[145] All of these attorneys in their private practice specialize in keeping corporations out of a court room.

Don't forget about suing the F.A.A., they need to be held accountable as well. In Congressional testimony acting F.A.A. Administrator Daniel Elwell said he would need $1.8 billion a year to properly oversee aviation manufacturing. Suing the F.A.A. for 15 years of inadequate protection to the flying public amounts to $27 billion, settling for anything less and the federal government will continue a path of destroying us, into the foreseeable future.

It is my opinion that Boeing is going to do the minimum required by the F.A.A. to get the 737 MAX flying again (and the F.A.A. wants them selling again quickly, to inflate the U.S. GDP), and the end situation with Boeing and the general public will be worse than where we are at now.

If the F.A.A. ungrounds the Boeing 737 MAX before other country's regulatory authorities do, then if anyone of them find something else to ground the fleet again, it would be embarrassing for U.S. corporations and our government in a foreseeable future.

Boeing is going to be used as a case study for the next couple of generations, how profits were put above customer safety. Professors will have so much to discuss with students: what a catastrophe the

---

[145] Business Insider, "Boeing Has Friends in High Places, Thanks to Its 737 Crash Czar", Tom Schoenberg, Julie Johnsson and Peter Robinson, 7/20/2019

Public Relations made of Boeing's response to both airplane crashes; how compartmentalizing groups inside a company can lead to tragedy because information is not shared; downsizing your workforce and at the same time contracting out to low paid overseas workers have real world consequences on the quality of units produced, etc..

23. GLOSSARY

    I've included terms and abbreviations common in aviation that I use in my book. When I was learning how to teach, one of the other students was given a task to explain aviation mnemonics, and he went off topic and let all of us know there are 23 different FAA's in the world, and only 1 relates to aviation. Any reader should use my glossary if they are confused about terminology.

A320NEO	The first A320NEO was delivered 25 January 2016, since then over 700 have been delivered by Airbus in 2019, it is a narrow body commercial airliner. Either engine option, a CFM International LEAP 1A or a Pratt & Whitney PW1000G engine, reduces fuel burn by 15% and decreases maintenance costs by almost 20%
A&P	**Airframe and Powerplant** License, many individuals have this license. It will authorize them to work on any aircraft system and return an aircraft to airworthy condition. Some foreign countries refer to these types of individuals as engineers
AC	**Advisory Circular**, an F.A.A. published document on how to achieve a certain result if followed, strictly voluntary
AD	**Airworthiness Directive**, The F.A.A. issues these documents when a safety of flight issue occurs, it forces operators to comply with the instructions in it. Besides specifying exactly what it applies to (not only make and model of aircraft, but usually includes the serial numbers affected as well), and a timeframe of when it has to be completed
ADC	**Air Data Computer**, new digital technology that replaces an old barometric altimeter. The

	original barometric altimeters use a bellows and mechanical linkages to show the pilot their altitude
ADI	**Attitude Directional Indicator**, instrument that shows the pitch and roll of the aircraft to the pilots
ADS-B	**Automatic Dependence Surveillance – Broadcast**, in essence, a system that broadcast its exact 3-D location and speed without human interaction. Many ground vehicle fleets use something similar to ADS-B to track company cars and trucks, where they are in real-time, and monitor how long they are stationary. For U.S. aircraft they typically employ GPS/WAAS for an accurate position source, and a transmitter to broadcast the position to Air Traffic Control. In Europe, they do not require a very accurate navigation source, so their implementation is different from what the U.S. requires
ADIRU	**Air Data Inertial Reference Unit**, it combines the Air Data Computer with an Inertial Reference Unit, along with a few extra functions added in. Before GPS it would calculate the aircraft's position within 1 nm for every hour of flight, nowadays it usually incorporates an internal GPS to give a very precise location (Airbus combines both an ADC and IRU into one unit)
AFM	**Aircraft Flight Manual**, a very long document included with all aircraft manufactured. At time of manufacture, it describes all of the systems installed, along with a lot of information useful to pilots
AGE	**Aircraft Ground Equipment**, normally this refers to any equipment on wheels that is used to service aircraft, such as hydraulic carts, or

	AC/DC Power carts, etc. (Ladder stands and like items are not normally thought of AGE.)
AMM	**Aircraft Maintenance Manual**, this document is used by maintenance and has sections numbered after the ATA (Air Transport Association) codes associated with all the sub-systems on an aircraft. Published by the manufacturer for a specific Make and Model aircraft, different airframe serial numbers will have different effectivity numbers on the bottom of each page
AND	**Automatic Nose Down**, a Pitch Trim command provided to the electric motor that controls the horizontal stabilizer to physically move up, so the aircraft moves in the opposite direction, and the aircraft nose pitches down
ANU	**Automatic Nose Up**, a Pitch Trim command provided to the electric motor that controls the horizontal stabilizer to move down, so the aircraft moves in the opposite direction, and the aircraft nose pitches up
AOA	**Angle of Attack**, is basically associated with aircraft stall, it's the point at which there is no lift on the wings. The critical angle of attack provides maximum lift, however if a fixed wing airplane exceeds this, lift is decreased dramatically, i.e. the aircraft goes into a stall. Many things will affect when the aircraft goes into a stall, such as airspeed, its weight, center of gravity, or a change in the direction of airflow (winds aloft change direction and speed). But it will always stall if the aircraft exceeds the same critical angle of attack. An AOA system on an aircraft will have a moveable sensor on the outside of the fuselage, with a display of AOA information to the pilot in the cockpit

A/P	**Autopilot**, standard shortened version to act like a mnemonic device on airplane paperwork
Appliance	In aviation any item that is not integral to the engine, propeller, or the airframe is an "appliance". It has nothing to do with devices found in a home's kitchen or laundry. Examples of an aircraft appliance would be an avionics box, an alternator, instrument, brakes, etc.
AR	**Airworthiness Representative**, a member of the ODA team, selected and paid by his/her employer, who submits data they certify to a manager from their company
ASI	**Airworthiness Safety Inspector**, a position in the F.A.A. created so an individual can oversee aircraft operation, maintenance, and manufacturing
ASRS	**Aviation Safety Reporting System**, a database maintained by NASA. Pilots can report anything related to aviation they determine is safety related, and NASA scrubs any identifying information from those reports, and then publishes it on their site without editing
ATC	**Air Traffic Control**, uses radar to identify where an aircraft is located, and VHF radio communication with pilots to maintain separation. English is the primary language for ATC for the whole world. In regions where there is no international traffic, then the Air Traffic Controllers speak in the local language. The FAA controls only U.S. airspace. In Europe they have 37 different ATC networks (almost each country has their own)
ATE	**Automatic Test Equipment**, most bench electronic test equipment can be computer controlled, and when they are used in conjunction

Avionics	with each other and controlled by software (like LabView), they form an ATE test station Any aircraft electronics is considered to be "avionics". In a related note, when working for an airline, anything with a wire on it is considered to be the Avionics Technician's responsibility
B/U	**Back-Up**, normally when there are two identical systems and only one is used at a time, the second system can be considered Back-Up. Exceptions to this general rule occurs when a power source (battery) is used power avionics, then that battery is considered Back-Up
C.A.A.	**Civil Aviation Authority**, for New Zeeland, very similar to the F.A.A. but only regulates their aviation community
Category III	When landing a plane, runways will be assigned a category by the F.A.A. depending on the navigation signals being used by an aircraft. For Category III, aircraft need their equipment certified, and the flight crews have to be current as well

Runway	Visual Range	Decision Height
Category I	More than 200 ft.	2,600 ft.
Category II	100-200 ft.	1,200-2,400 ft.
Category III A	Less than 100 ft.	Less than 700 ft.
Category III B	Less than 50 ft.	150-700 ft.
Category III C	0 ft.	None

CDO	**Certified Design Organization**, an idea to remove all F.A.A. oversight over airplane manufacturers, so the process of creating a new product can be sped up by having one company

	certify everything they make without F.A.A. oversight
CEO	**Chief Executive Officer**, it is a position where the person is appointed to run the company, and he/she makes decisions that affect everyone in that organization on a day to day basis
CFM	**CFM International** makes the LEAP engines that power the 737 MAX and A320 NEO aircraft. It's a joint venture between American GE Aviation and French Safran Aircraft Engines. The 737 MAX uses the LEAP 1A engine, whereas the A320NEO uses the LEAP 1B engine
CG	**Center of Gravity**, if you were able to balance an airplane like you do a pencil on a finger, that point is the aircraft's center of gravity. It is allowed to shift within certain guidelines, depending on fuel load, cargo, and passengers
CPR	**Cardiopulmonary Resuscitation**, is an emergency technique that combines chest compressions with moth-to-mouth ventilation, trying to keep a person's brain alive by giving the body air and circulating its blood
CPU	**Central Processing Unit**, the heart and brains of a computer. In avionics almost everything has a CPU, even in a VHF Radio it is possible to find 3 CPU's. Today Intel sells a single chip with 16 cores inside of a single CPU, and each one of those cores can run 4 different programs at the same time through partitioning. A state-of-the-art Autopilot Computer will have 3 CPU's, each made from a different manufacture, running the same type of software in case one goes bad
CVR	**Cockpit Voice Recorder**, mandated to be installed by the FAA in certain types of aircraft, records most audio, for a minimum of 120 minutes. Everything over the pilot or copilot's

	microphone is recorded, and there is an area microphone that picks up all audible noise in the cockpit
D.O.D.	**Department of Defense**, military and civilian employees that comprise our national defense
EASA	**European Union Aviation Safety Agency**, Based in Cologne, Germany, is an agency of the European Union (EU) and has jurisdiction over new aircraft type certificates and other design-related airworthiness approvals for aircraft, engines, propellers, and parts; it began around 2003
EFIS	**Electronic Flight Information System**, its essentially a glass cockpit today, where all of the flight information is displayed on LCD's
DER	**Designated Engineering Representative**, the F.A.A. will authorize an individual to certify and approve documentation, as they longer have enough personnel to do all of the functions that small aviation companies need to accomplish. These individuals are normally self-employed and are separate from an Airworthiness Representative (AR) on an ODA team
F.A.A.	**Federal Aviation Administration**, regulate all aspects of civil aviation, it had its foundation created in 1958
FCC	**Flight Control Computer**, used on 737 aircraft to control aircraft flight surfaces, mainly by autopilot
FERS	**Federal Employee Retirement System**, government employees since 1983 are enrolled in this civil service retirement program
FDR	**Flight Data Recorder**, many refer to this as a "black box" although they are always painted bright orange, with a couple of reflective stripes. It records many parameters of the aircraft, so it

	can be analyzed after a crash to see what happened
FDAU	**Flight Data Acquisition Unit**, most modern aircraft have a FDAU positioned electrically in front of the FDR, it receives all of the data first, and makes a copy onto a removable QAR unit while sending the data to the FDR
EFC	**Elevator Feel Computer**, used in Boeing commercial airplanes, whenever there is no longer a direct connection between the pilot's yoke and the elevators, this computer applies tension so the pilot manually flying the aircraft will notice little difference from previous models
FSB	**Flight Standardization Board**, a panel of ASI's who decide on what type of training is required for pilots when a new Type Certificate is issued for an airframe (that is the same thing as a birth certificate for an aircraft – can't fly without it)
FOQA	**Flight Operations Quality Assurance** Program, it is a program where management uses QAR data, after scrubbing personal identification of it, to see if pilots are putting down the landing gear to soon, too late, etc.
"g"	Gravity, one "g" is the force a human feels when they walk upon the Earth. Above the Earth, spacecraft and aircraft can exert on the body more than the forces felt normally while walking on the ground. At 2 "g's" your weight is essentially double, you "feel" twice as heavy, and it takes effort to move your arms. At 3 "g's" besides feeling 3 times your weight, forces act on the body differently, higher levels will cause humans to black out, at extremes – death
GAO	**Government Accounting Office**, they provide auditing of various U.S. federal entities

GDP	**Gross Domestic Product**, every country produces goods and services, the total is reported annually as the nation's GDP
GO-AROUND	All standard approach procedures pilots use to land at airports will have a missed-approach feature (**Go-Around**). If for any reason a landing approach is aborted, like a deer is on the runway, then there is a path to follow to a referenced point in the sky. Pilots fly around this reference point in a racetrack pattern until they are allowed to try and land again
GPS	**Global Positioning System**, the U.S. has 24 active satellites used for navigation. Each satellite is approximately 22,000 miles high and they circle the Earth twice each day. Every satellite broadcasts on the exact same frequency. How a GPS receiver tells which satellite is which, is done by the Doppler Effect. As the satellite approaches you, its frequency will increase (radio waves compressed), as it departs from you its frequency will decrease. Each satellite has an atomic clock to keep precision timing. A GPS receiver needs to have 3 satellites in view to triangulate its position. A fourth satellite is required for RAIM (Receiver Autonomous Integrity Monitoring developed so a GPS receiver can tell if it is outside of its normal accuracy). A fifth satellite is required to obtain a vertical height accuracy
GPWS	**Ground Proximity Warning System**, a way to prevent an aircraft from Controlled Flight Into Terrain (CFIT). Using GPS as precision source of where you are, along with a topographical database of terrain and obstructions (tall buildings, cell towers, etc.), it basically prevents

pilots from unknowingly flying an aircraft into the ground

HDG	**Heading**, will be which way is the aircraft pointing. There is magnetic heading, it's the most commonly used heading source, as most charts use magnetic heading as a reference point. The aircraft will use a magnetic compass system to display aircraft heading. However magnetic heading changes over time, usually around 1 degree every year; because the magnetic poles of the Earth change position every year. All charts and runway markers will be updated about every 8 years. And depending on where you are located, magnetic north can change as much as 2 degrees every year. For more sophisticated avionics, such as AHRS or IRU, a pilot can select TRUE heading, which eliminates the changes in the Earth magnetic poles
IAS	**Indicated Air Speed**, this is the speed a pilot will reference, when calculating flight profiles. There are many types of aircraft airspeed, True Airspeed, Calculated Airspeed, and Ground Speed, but IAS is basic for pilots, it is the air pressure sensed at the pitot tubes
IATA	**International Air Transport Association,** it is now a lobbying organization for 80% of the world's airlines. They not only do lobby activities at over 100 government entities; they are also a clearing house for the airlines they represent
ICAO	**International Civil Aviation Organization**, created in 1944. An organization which has no rule making authority, but, influences the aviation community world-wide through its research and forward-looking ideas. They employ under their "umbrella" inspectors from all nations, to do ASI functions in countries that

	do not have the infrastructure to support a regulating body
IG	**Inspector General**, government entities rely on their own internal IG departments to deliver audits and investigations that will be fact driven and free from their parent organization
IRU	**Inertial Reference Unit**, gives both attitude and heading. Originally, they used gyroscopes and accelerometers for attitude and heading, they also provide present position and speed. Now laser ring gyros have replaced mechanically spinning gyros, the accelerometers are now so accurate they can tell your Latitude to within 1 mile by sensing the Earth's rotation. No external sensors are required. Present position must be entered manually to start. An IRU can drift 1 mile every hour, and still be considered good
Knots	Term used to measure speed, it is referenced to the speed it takes to travel one nautical mile (1 knot = 1.15078 mph)
Mach	Mach is the speed of sound at sea level = 767 mph. Air density is quite compact at sea level, so as the altitude increase, the Mach number will change as well
Mach Trim	**Mach Trim**, is a system used by the 737 MAX 8 aircraft when the speed is between 0.61 and 0.86 Mach, used to counter the speeds when high speed occurs in manual flight
MCAS	**Maneuvering Characteristics Augmentation System**, any AOA sensor will trigger this system to move the horizontal stabilizer to avoid an aircraft stall automatically without pilot intervention
MFD	**Multi-Function Display**, typically in smaller aircraft there will be one in the center of the instrument panel, for bigger aircraft each pilot

	will have one. These really are multi-function displays, showing chart information, checklists, ability to show a flight plan, and even sometimes acting as a moving map display. More expensive displays in General Aviation will have a GPS, VOR/ILS navigation, and communication equipment integrated within them
NG	**Next Generation**, Boeing uses this to describe the third generation 737 airplane
NTSB	**National Transportation Safety Board**, U.S. government agency responsible for investigating civil transportation crashes (car/rail/air). Allowed to find root causes of accidents, and make recommendations, it, however, has no power to implement anything it deems important
ODA	**Organization Designation Authorization**, created by the F.A.A. in 2005, it lets aircraft manufacturers inspect themselves. F.A.A. inspectors designate inspectors at the manufacturer to take their place, each inspector designates approximately 40 AR's, of which he/she oversees
OSHA	**Occupational Safety and Health Administration**, U.S. agency responsible for workplace safety and health
QA	**Quality Assurance**, Inspectors in this department not only verify that parts, repairs, and modifications are acceptable and airworthy, they are responsible for most aviation paperwork. (Quality Control is a limited term; applications are mostly to verify a component is correct)
QAR	**Quick Access Recorder**, normally has an access point for the flight crew to pull out a removable media device full of data after a flight, and insert a blank media device

PASS	**Profession Aviation System Specialists Union**, its members are mostly made up of F.A.A. air traffic controllers and airworthiness safety inspectors
PIC	**Pilot-in-Command**, in aircraft, the person who occupies the left seat of the cockpit is the PIC, he/she is normally called Captain
PFD	**Primary Flight Display**, it normally combines multiple displays into one place directly in front of the pilots. In small aircraft that are rated for a single pilot, normally only one PFD is installed. In instances where it requires two pilots to fly an aircraft (larger aircraft) each pilot will have their own PFD. People will say an aircraft has a glass cockpit if it has a PFD and MFD
QRH	**Quick Reference Guide**, used by professional pilots in commercial aircraft. It is a handy reference for the different systems installed in the aircraft, along with Non-Normal Checklists (Abnormal / Emergency Checklists)
RALT	**Radio Altimeter**, a device that uses radar principles to determine the exact feet above ground level, it will blank out after 2,000 – 2,500 feet, because it is not to be used above those altitudes
RTCA	**Radio Technical Commission for Aeronautics**, it publishes standards for aviation
SAE	**Society of Automotive Engineers**, originally a body that concerned itself with setting standards for the automotive industry in the U.S., that is no longer the case. Many other organizations will create standards and house them at SAE, who then sells them to the general public
SB	**Service Bulletin**, any manufacturer of aircraft or components thereof, will publish a voluntary recommendation for their product. Users of these

	airplanes or "appliances" then decide whether to implement them or not
SIC	**Second-in-Command**, the person who occupies the right seat of the cockpit is the SIC, he/she is normally called First Officer
SID	**Standard Instrument Departure**, a chart depicting a standardize route to follow when departing a major airport
SMYD	**Stall Management / Yaw Damper** Computer, used in commercial aviation to alert pilots to and impending stall, as well as providing controls to the rudder tab on the tail to avoid it from fishtailing in the sky.
SOCAC	**Safety Oversight and Certification Advisory Committee**, Department of Transportation created a committee to understand issues confronting aviation in the next 5 years (from March 2019), a minimum of 11 and maximum of 20 members is allowed, all voluntary, unpaid positions (political in nature)
STAR	**Standard Terminal Approach Route**, an IFR navigation approach to a runway at an airport, using many different navigational means to achieve landing on a runway
STAB TRIM	An electrical motor turns the horizontal stabilizer, the system that does this is called STAB TRIM, sometimes it is referred to as Pitch Trim
TAB	**Technical Advisory Board**, committee created to ensure MCAS software is correct before it is approved to install into the 737 MAX, second set of eyes over the F.A.A.
TAWS	**Terrain Awareness and Warning System**, it is basically a second generation of GPWS, and is required to be installed into turbine-powered aircraft with six or more passenger seats.

	Sometimes it is referred to as enhanced GPWS (eGPWS). It incorporates a forward-looking feature, and is active even when landing, along with providing windshear alerts
TCAS	**Traffic Collision Avoidance System** (sometimes referred to as Traffic Alert and Collision Avoidance System), TCAS I is mandated for aircraft that fly under the regulations contained in 14 CFR Part 135 and carry less than 30 passengers. TCAS II is required for aircraft that carry 30 passengers or more. TCAS is independent from ATC; it provides surveillance around the aircraft and is interfaced with a Mode-S transponder. Basically, TCAS provides a similar display to the pilots, that is given to an ATC controller on his/her radar screen. TCAS I can only generate traffic alerts. TCAS II can generate both traffic alerts and resolution advisories. TCAS equipment which is capable of processing ADS-B messages may use this information to enhance the performance of TCAS, using techniques known as "hybrid surveillance". Using reception of ADS-B OUT messages from other aircraft will reduce the rate at which the TCAS equipment interrogates other aircraft. TCAS consists of a computer unit, Mode-S transponder, and a cockpit display to the pilots. (TCAS Change 7.1 is adding functionality between TCAS computer and ADS-B equipment, improves logic of giving a resolution advisories by incorporating ADS-B messages; required in Europe by 1/1/2017.)
V1	Speed of no return, once this speed is achieved as the airplane is on the runway accelerating for flight, if an airplane achieves V1 speed it is

	committed to go airborne, no amount of brake pressure or thrust reversers can stop it
V2	Common term in aviation to refer to a speed an aircraft needs to achieve before they are allowed to maneuver the aircraft while airborne. The V2 speed will be different for the varied types of airframes, small general aviation planes weighing 1,200 lbs. will have a much lower speed than a narrow body commercial airliner
Vr	Speed needed for rotation (take-off) is Vr
UAV	**Unmanned Aerial Vehicles**, simple version is a drone that has 4 propellers and is controlled by hand using a transmitter (a good example would be a DJI Phantom), However many large companies envision a time when they build aircraft, pilotless, that can transport people, like an "air taxi"
UTC	**Universal Time Coordinated**, it refers to the time on the zero or Greenwich meridian. Greenwich, England sits on this prime meridian of the world. Before 1972 this was called Greenwich Mean Time (GMT), pilots also call this ZULU time. So, aviation can be synchronized wherever an aircraft is on Earth by UTC time
VFR	**Visual Flight Rules**, used by pilots when they fly below cloud cover and can see where he/she is flying. No instrumentation for navigation is required. Visual Metrological Conditions (VMC) is what governs whether a pilot can fly without IFR instrumentation

Made in the USA
Columbia, SC
29 August 2019